Experiences of Counse

learning network
west

Experiences of Counsellor Training: challenge, surprise and change

Edited by

Val Harding Davies
Geof Alred
Kathy Hunt

and

Graham Davies

First published 2004 by
PALGRAVE MACMILLAN
Houndmills, Basingstoke, Hampshire RG21 6XS and
175 Fifth Avenue, New York, N.Y. 10010
Companies and representatives throughout the world

PALGRAVE MACMILLAN is the global academic imprint of the Palgrave Macmillan division of St. Martin's Press LLC and of Palgrave Macmillan Ltd. Macmillan® is a registered trademark in the United States, United Kingdom and other countries. Palgrave is a registered trademark in the European Union and other countries.

ISBN 1–4039–2186–5

This book is printed on paper suitable for recycling and made from fully managed and sustained forest sources.

A catalogue record for this book is available from the British Library.

10   9   8   7   6   5   4   3   2   1
13 12 11 10 09 08 07 06 05 04

Typeset in Great Britain by
Aarontype Ltd, Easton, Bristol

Printed in China

Contents

Preface

Counselling training is distinctively a product of the late-twentieth century development. Its key features were probably initiated by Carl Rogers and his colleagues at the University of Chicago in the 1940s. It is an educational experience which is typically based in a university or college, and shares some of the characteristics of other applied or vocational courses: learning about theory and research, developing skills, undertaking placements that involve working with clients, being assessed, being a member of a peer group, reading, writing. But in other ways it is a highly unusual type of educational experience. There are perhaps two aspects of counsellor training that mark it out as different from courses in other areas of 'people work', such as nursing, teaching and social work. The first is that counselling trainees are explicitly required to examine their own sense of self, identity, and ways of relating to others. This is not the kind of learning and maturing process that occurs in other professions, where a trainee is perhaps faced for the first time with suffering, or other people from very different cultural and social backgrounds. In counselling, the 'work on self' permeates all elements of training, on a daily basis. This can be an experience that can be frightening and disruptive, as well as exciting and formative. The second unusual aspect of counselling training is that, very early on, the trainee is put in a position of working solo, with a high degree of autonomy, with clients. In contrast to other types of training, there are relatively few possibilities for observing or 'shadowing' experienced practitioners, or for co-working.

The experience of being a trainee can have an intense quality. The course community becomes an arena in which different dimensions of the trainee's capacity to be with others are played out in multiple current relationships. The encouragement is always there to reflect on what is happening, to find significance, make meaning. At the same time, these fellow trainees are a group of people who are being faced by the same challenges, and are a source of help and support. On many courses, the intensity of the group experience may be built up by such means as unstructured community meetings, residentials and peer assessment. Members of a counselling course may learn things about themselves, and form friendship and professional networks, which last a lifetime. But there may be a cost, in the strain felt by pre-existing family and other relationships in the 'real' world, and in a sense of disappointment when the end of the course does not lead on to meaningful work opportunities. Many of the contributors in this book vividly explore their own personal journey into and through the experience of being a member of a counselling course community.

Another facet of counsellor training which is expressed many times in these stories is the thirst for learning that is associated with the process of becoming a counsellor. The potential knowledge base that may be relevant to the work of a counsellor is potentially immense, and certainly far too much to cover in a course which might typically last for two or three years. There is a rich and extensive literature in the field of counselling and psychotherapy, and the majority of practitioners will find new domains for personal learning and study throughout their career. It may be that the emphasis on self-awareness that permeates the culture of counselling in Britain makes this kind of reading more meaningful: whatever is being read is matched against personal experience, or the experience of specific clients with whom the counsellor has worked.

The chapters in this book illustrate, too, some of the tensions within contemporary counselling practice. One of the main areas of tension is associated, in my view, with the over-individualized concept of the person that is presented within person-centred and psychodynamic theories and their many variants. The theoretical and conceptual core of most counselling training centres around learning how to work therapeutically with 'inner self' of the client. However, a course community may function as a microcosm of a wider culture in which categories of difference, in areas such as gender, social class, age, race, sexual orientation and disability, are crucially important to a person's life and the identity he or she might construct. While counselling courses may provide spaces for reflection on such differences, and the power imbalances that come with them, an individualized way of thinking about persons allows few resources for structuring and exploring these issues. Quite often, course communities can get stuck when such issues emerge.

A further tension that arises in the writing of some contributors to this book concerns the role of theory itself in counselling practice.

On the whole, the majority of courses train people in a single model of practice, whereas the majority of practitioners describe themselves as eclectic or integrative, and combine models as necessary in their everyday work with clients. These stories of people in training reflect some of the dilemmas associated with the core theory versus integration debate. How can a trainee make a commitment to a single theoretical model when so many other plausible models exist?

Once trained in a core model, what kind of work needs to be undertaken by a practitioner to develop a personal approach that integrates ideas and techniques form other models? It may be that the tensions over theoretical 'purity' that surface in this book are a reflection of a current state of transition within the counselling profession in relation to the role and purpose of 'theory'. In the past, the kind of underlying assumptions that dominated the profession made it inevitable that training and practice would be organized around major 'brand name' theories. We are moving rapidly toward a situation, I would argue, in which the 'common factors' that cut across all theoretical models are being more widely recognized, and a postmodern scepticism around any set of ideas that claims to offer a total explanatory framework, is coming to prevail. It may be that, if another edition of this book were to be written in ten years from now, we would find that trainees were writing about their engagement with theory in quite a different manner.

What is the value in collecting students' accounts of counselling training? Where is the interest in reading such accounts? From a research perspective, these accounts enable a form of 'narrative knowing' that could never be matched by any study that used questionnaires, coded interview transcripts and the like. Reading through this set of stories makes it possible to understand what the experience of counselling training is like, from the point of view of the trainee. Taken together, the chapters offer a rich, 'multi-storied' account of this area of life. From a professional perspective, this book represents a unique historical record, a snapshot of what training is like now. The book documents a form of practice that is changing – courses evolve, are closed – and is in some respects unique to counselling in Britain. A profession with a strong identity needs to document and understand its history, and the different traditions that may exist within that history. I suspect that people who have completed counsellor training in North America and Europe might regard the narratives within this book as strangely 'personal', and perhaps chaotic, in comparison to their own experiences. Colleagues in Australia and New Zealand, by contrast, might find much that is familiar to them. It is only by taking the trouble to record such stories that we can engage in such conversations, and build a deeper appreciation of the forms of professional practice that have evolved within different cultural communities.

I would like to thank the contributors to this book, for their willingness to share their experiences – some joyful, some angry – with a wider audience. I would also like to thank Val Harding Davies, Geof Alred, Kathy Hunt and Graham Davies, for their perseverance in bringing this project to fruition. They have each given long service to two of the pioneering university-based counselling courses in England (at Keele and Durham), and they know how important these stories are.

John McLeod
Dundee
February 2003

1

Introduction

Val Harding Davies, Geof Alred, Kathy Hunt and Graham Davies

Introduction

This book is an anthology of stories told by a group of people not long after they had completed counsellor training. Their stories are about being a trainee, the effects and outcomes of training, both positive and negative, and the richness and diversity of the training experience. The authors reflect a variety of backgrounds in terms of age, gender, ethnic identity and life history. The courses they followed include person-centred, psychodynamic and broadly humanistic approaches, and have in common two related beliefs: individuals have resources to change for the better which can be realized to some degree with the help of another person, a counsellor; and the heart of therapeutic helping is the relationship between counsellor and client. In the concluding chapter, we identify themes in the various accounts and comment on lessons that might be drawn by current and future trainees and trainers.

Counsellor training is often a time of significant change. Were it not so there would exist an odd contradiction and tension between what is claimed a person might gain by becoming a client – help in living more resourcefully, help in living with less disturbance and distress – and what counsellors claim they offer. It would suggest that counselling is essentially a technical or theoretical activity. It is certainly the case that trainees do become more skilled and do acquire theoretical perspectives to guide practice. But as well, many come to feel and think differently, both personally and professionally. They change in ways that go beyond technique and theory. Increased

1

knowledge, understanding and competence in being a professional helper become rooted in an altered sense of self. This book is about such changes and the experiences from which they come. We begin our introduction with two illustrations from the experience of recently qualified counsellors.

The experience of counsellor training

'I want to find out what I am like'. This was an ambition of someone at the beginning of training. Some months after completing the course, the same person, now qualified, declares with conviction – 'I now *know* I can counsel'. Her self knowledge is fundamentally different from the uncertain belief in herself that led to the decision to train more than two years previously. The change is more than increased confidence and competence, she *does* know better what she is like. What she can do to help others flows from her identity as a counsellor.

An MA student, a trained nurse familiar with human anatomy including brain structure, studies for her thesis the use of imagery in counselling seriously and terminally ill children. The project gathers momentum – she introduces imagery into her counselling practice, she makes contact with other counsellors and therapists experienced in working this way, she reads widely, she infects non-counselling colleagues with her enthusiasm. In carrying out an exercise to meet an academic requirement, she is changing. The change is felt, lived out in her professional life. She knows she now has much more to give the children and is herself reinvigorated in an area of work that takes a heavy emotional toll. Half way through the project, she refers to the right brain hemisphere, as the site of the imagination, and declares with great glee and surprise 'I didn't *know* it was there!'

These fragments of two counsellors' stories, in essence about knowing, touch upon themes of immense importance in counselling and counsellor training, and of deep significance to their respective authors – themes to do with personal change, counselling technique and practice, self awareness and self knowledge, linking and separating the personal and the professional, taking the fruits of counsellor training into other contexts, into other areas of life. Such themes and many more and the experiences that make them real will be familiar to numerous other counsellors whose training remains fresh, either by virtue of being recent or through success in maintaining what has been called the 'living reality' of being a counsellor (Connor, 1995).

Another theme of the two fragments is the telling. These recently qualified counsellors are giving voice to their experience, communicating to another its significance for them. They are also communicating with themselves as they know that doing so is an integral part of how they have achieved the hard won benefits and lessons of counsellor training – telling the story is inseparable from living it. The chapters of this book go further than these fragments. They illustrate the themes of finding a voice as a counsellor and telling the story of counsellor training. Ten people present a personal view of their experience of training, written within three years of undertaking training. Collectively they offer a unique picture, albeit a partial one, of counsellor training in contemporary Britain, at a particular time in the history of the young profession of counselling. Each writes from within a particular social, cultural and economic context. The book is intended as a contribution to sustaining and making explicit the 'reality' of being a counsellor that training can bring to life, and that is the bedrock of the social value of counselling. It also illustrates the demands of training, and acknowledges the serious challenges facing counselling as a profession. It invites the reader to enter eleven personal worlds, to share something of what training was like, of what really mattered, to learn what is the upshot, personally and professionally, and to appreciate the contexts from which the trainees approached their training and the transactions and tensions between the training and all other parts of their lives.

As the chapters amply reveal, no two trainees have the same experience, or reflect on it in the same way. In an important sense each trainee follows a different course, as they bring their own unique selves, their own preoccupations and priorities to the formality and discipline of a course structure and content, and join a unique mix of participants, fellow trainees and staff, for the duration of the course.

Alongside uniqueness of individual experience, there is, of course, much common ground. It comes from the circumstances of training – from being in the same cohort, working with the same tutors, studying in the same institution, or practising within the same therapeutic orientation. It comes also from having had similar life experiences. As a British Association of Counselling (BAC,[1] 1993) membership survey revealed, counsellors are not a random sample

---

[1] The British Association for Counselling changed its name to British Association for Counselling and Psychotherapy in 2000.

of the population. They often share personal qualities, and to some degree fall into recognizable sociological groupings. Thus we believe the following chapters reflect also themes that will be familiar to others involved in counsellor training. A trainer, for instance, may see the fruits of her labours manifest in these trainees' experiences; a current trainee may see herself reflected, or find herself challenged or surprised; a would-be trainee may glimpse what is to come, may have her apprehensions assuaged, her anticipation aroused, she may see a little way into her future. Someone who has been a client may understand better, or differently, the experience of therapy. Colleagues, friends, family may gain insight into their experience of relating to someone undergoing training.

By bringing together a collection of first hand accounts from newly trained counsellors, we seek also to demonstrate to a wider audience what is well known to trainers and trainees – the experience of training can be immensely rich, challenging, exciting and sometimes painful, and its long-term consequences very significant. In its annual report for 1995, the British Association for Counselling (BAC) declared a commitment to the broad social value of a flourishing counselling profession. This book seeks to contribute to this project by emphasizing that the effects of training, what people take from it, and the commitment to continue personal and professional development beyond training have the potential to enrich the communities and settings within which counsellors live and work. An essential element of such a contribution is a critical stance towards training. Through and beyond the immediate experience of trainees, which can be engrossing and deeply personal, we seek to identify the costs, as well as the benefits, the curse as well as the blessing, of becoming a counsellor.

We hope that this collection of chapters will be of interest and value to current trainees, to trainers and to anyone whose professional or personal life is affected by counselling. We hope it will be of especial interest to those who are in training, contemplating training or are soon to embark on a course.

The professional framework of counsellor training

Professional frameworks put into practice beliefs about the best way to prepare and equip a person for the arduous and demanding work of counselling. They reflect theoretical understanding of human change and learning, philosophical issues concerned with basic human values, and issues to do with professional standards, accountability and ethical conduct.

According to the British Association for Counselling and Psychotherapy (BACP), for example, a professional counsellor training course is organized within a framework consisting of eight elements. These are:

• a detailed admissions policy and selection procedure
• opportunities for ongoing self-development
• the stipulation that students undertake client work
• regular supervision during the course
• structured opportunities for skills training
• a thorough grounding in counselling theory with special reference to the course core theoretical model
• opportunities for professional development
• proper assessment and evaluation procedures.

Further detail of this framework can be found in Dryden, Horton and Mearns (1995) and Dryden and Thorne (1991). Details of other professional bodies that set training standards can be found in Bor and Palmer (2001) and Schapira (2000).

The main elements of training are counselling theory, developing counselling skills and techniques and opportunities for personal development. The curriculum is delivered using a variety of learning methods, and trainers aim to integrate these elements to provide coherence in the training experience.

Trainees find their own path through the course, they are both in the company of others and they are apart. They are making a personal journey of self-exploration and change, creating their own signposts and way stations, and in doing so they are confronting and accepting the moral and professional responsibilities conferred by training, they are joining a community of practitioners. As the process unfolds, they are more or less conscious of what is going on, and all the while encouraged to reflect and become more aware. Seasoned therapists often report that their motives for entering training are not fully known until after, sometimes a long time after, the training has ended (Norcross and Guy, 1989).

The trainer, for his or her part, stands somewhere between the professional framework and the trainees' experiences. Their task is to provide facilitation, safety and opportunities for serious learning. It is a daunting task, not least because 'if things go well they will not go smoothly' (Dryden and Thorne, 1991, p. 3), as several of the following chapters reveal. Self-exploration leads to new discoveries, often in long neglected psychological terrain. It can be painful work, and what is discovered can be uncomfortable, distressing or frightening, as well as exciting, welcome, liberating, energizing.

In the following chapters, the professional framework and context, the trainers' input and influence, and indeed some of the trainers' own experiences, are evident and implicit in how trainees saw, felt and thought about it all. The contributors were asked for personal accounts within which the course as provided, its content, schedules, demands and practices, could be detected by the careful reader. The brief to them was open: to write about their training experience in terms they felt did it justice and which would be accessible to a wide audience. The chapters arise out of and contribute to dialogue among trainees, between trainers and trainees, and in the wider circles of trainees' lives. They are also conversations with self, slow-motion snapshots of conversations begun and set to continue. Each story gives a sense of the idiosyncratic nature of the journey undertaken.

Finding a voice

It is widely recognized that the counsellor as a person is the heart of therapeutic helping (Norcross and Guy, 1989) and an important part of becoming a counsellor is the process of finding an authentic voice, of knowing yourself as best you can. Within training, activities such as keeping a learning journal, writing case reports, essays, research reports, learning and personal development statements, along with countless conversations, all contribute to finding a voice as a counsellor.

The chapters stem both from the professional motivation to achieve transparency in the eyes of all who are affected by counselling, both inside and outside communities of practitioners, and from the belief that telling our story is one way, perhaps the central way, in which we become who we are. Each chapter is introduced by an abstract to assist the reader in appreciating both the uniqueness of each training experience and how individuals responded to the recurring themes of challenge, surprise and change. While there is much a prospective trainee can do to prepare her/himself for what lies ahead, training is often demanding and leads to unforeseen effects. One way to get the greatest benefit is to accept that the challenges of training will bring surprises and change, to expect the unexpected, and to engage as fully as one can with all that training offers and provokes. The contributors to this book did just that.

They also recognize that the impact of training continues to reverberate long after it is completed and have used the opportunity to write about their experience as part of their continuing development. For current and prospective trainees, it is hoped the stories that follow: will *challenge* motivations to become trained counsellors and expectations of training; will *surprise* by their richness, seriousness, honesty, and personal and professional significance; and will assist through reflection and comparison the *changes* that are the promise and price of counsellor training.

References

Bor, R. and Palmer, S. (eds) (2001) *A Beginner's Guide to Training in Counselling and Psychotherapy*, London: Sage.
British Association for Counselling (1993) Membership Survey, Rugby: BAC.
Connor, M. (1995) *Training the Counsellor*, London: Routledge, p. 20.
Dryden, W., Horton, I. and Mearns, D. (1995) *Issues in Professional Counsellor Training*, London: Cassell.
Dryden, W. and Thorne, B. (1991) *Training and Supervision for Counselling in Action*, London: Sage, p. 3.
Norcross, J. C. and Guy, J. D., 'Ten Therapists: the process of becoming and being', in W. Dryden and L. Spurling (1989) *On Becoming a Psychotherapist*, London: Tavistock/Routledge.
Schapira, S. K. (2000) *Choosing a Counselling or Psychotherapy Training: A Practical Guide*, London: Routledge.

2

Picking up the Gauntlet

Van-Anh Tran

Van-Anh Tran gives a graphic account of how training to be a counsellor brought him face-to-face with two imposing challenges in his life's journey – first, confronting his cultural ethnicity and coming to appreciate fully the ramifications of what it means to be 'different', and second, wrestling with the tension and uncertainties surrounding the question of a significant career change. The pressure to choose between two polarized positions is vividly described, as well as the feeling of isolation generated by a sense of not belonging to either camp. The story of how he responded to these challenges is humanly and movingly unfolded.

In the beginning

This chapter is an account of a personal journey, of becoming the person I am and of my development as a counsellor. The experience of counsellor training is a central part of that journey. To write about the training experience is to describe how lessons learned in life were put to the test by the values, beliefs and practices embodied in it. It is also to convey that what was challenging and valuable about training rests upon a context of influences from my family and early adulthood. Hence a central theme is the tension between what I brought to the course and what I took from it; a tension that was at times painful but was also the source of significant learning. To a large degree, the tension had its origins in a sense in being 'different' from others.

My mother is English and my father is Vietnamese. I was named Van-Anh out of respect for my grandmother who visited from Saigon when I was born in London in 1962. My upbringing was certainly very English, being educated at a public school, where I was largely unaware of my 'difference' in relation to my peers and teachers.

In fact, I remember aligning myself with white friends rather than with boys of other ethnic origins. I am not that visibly different from many white people, unless you care to look. And in fact people have often said (and still do) that they sometimes wonder if I had some 'foreign blood' in me. Colour did not seem to be an issue among family and friends. However, there were occasions when my somewhat partial view of my own identity was uncomfortably challenged. For example, when I was about seven years old, I was asked to write an account of 'what I had for dinner'. In my essay, I mentioned a condiment that was normally used at home, and that in my innocence I had assumed everybody knew about. When I got my piece of work back it had the Vietnamese words *nuoc mam* crossed out in red. I still think about this episode and the cumulative effects of racism, unconscious or not. Of course, I did not think in those terms then. I just thought I had written something 'wrong'. Looking back, however, I do remember wishing that I could look a little less 'foreign', that perhaps my nose could look a little more like my mum's and a little less like my father's. A later jolt to my self-perceptions came in my teens during the late 1970s, when I encountered a group of racist football fans on a train in London one Saturday. They did not harm me physically, but I knew to whom they directed their comments, as no one else was anywhere near to being a 'Paki' who should 'go home'. However, I was relieved I was not alone in the carriage. I recall that soon afterwards I became aware of the National Front, which was very visible in London at that time.

My attempts at leading what some call a 'colour-blind' life continued pretty successfully at university, where I studied psychology. I became interested in developmental and clinical psychology and especially psychotherapy. In particular, the teaching by the clinical psychologist David Smail was very challenging and stimulating. I began to think about a career in clinical psychology, and in order to pursue this I knew that I would need to gain significant work experience. I decided to train as a psychiatric nurse. It was my first, and so far only, major career mistake.

I knew it was a mistake right from the start. The last straw was my placement on a psychogeriatric ward where, in my view, the patients were treated in an undignified and often humiliating manner. I felt I would lose myself if I stayed in that environment, so I made a decision that felt like taking responsibility for my life for the first time. I resigned.

After a period of voluntary work, I became employed at a social services day centre for the elderly. As part of my continuing professional development, I undertook several counselling skills courses. I stayed in the centre for five years, learning a lot about working with people, about myself, and how I related to others.

Perhaps it was something to do with working in social services, but it was at this time I found that my political awareness was awakening. I began to attend meetings of the Socialist Workers' Party. However, I never joined and feel now that I may have been attracted to them because of a need to belong to something that was not part of the mainstream, a reflection of my sense that I did not 'belong' anywhere in particular. Ironically, my experience of race awareness training at that time pushed me further into a sense of alienation and difference. I was taught that I did not own my 'blackness' (due to internalized oppression, so I was told) while at the same time I was not being seen by my colleagues as anything other than white. The approach seemed to demand that I disown a part of my heritage. At that time I had not yet read in a book or experienced from another person anything that really made sense to me. I felt that my own journey to a way of identifying myself was going to be a difficult one.

After a period of employment in a night shelter for homeless people, I worked for six years in a residential rehabilitation project set up for people with mental health problems who, in the main, had been previously detained in the special hospital system. I began to learn about making therapeutic relationships with people, many of whom had been diagnosed as having a psychopathic personality disorder and who had led destructive and sometimes murderous lives. Over time I learned some hard lessons about my own limitations and in some cases the limits of therapeutic relationships. I began to realize that I wanted to train in counselling, both for the job I was in and possibly as a future career. I was becoming aware that I had potential to be a counsellor and that I found individual therapeutic work both rewarding and interesting. I successfully applied for training as a voluntary counsellor. It felt that I had thrown down the gauntlet to myself!

Becoming a counsellor

I was daunted at the prospect of doing counselling 'for real' and at the length of the core training to which I committed myself. The

18-month course consisted of one evening per week and whole day workshops. In common with many others, I had perceived counselling as a world inhabited predominantly by white middle-class, middle-aged women. My experience on the various 'counselling skills' courses had only served to reinforce this perception. So it was a pleasant surprise that the training group of about twenty had a number of black faces, a few men and a wide range of ages. I had high hopes that there would be opportunities for discourse on issues of race, gender, sexuality, disability, etc. There were individual workshops that concerned these issues. However, some of the group including me felt that these were somehow 'added on', and then put aside rather than kept as 'live' issues to be integrated into the teaching and value base of the training. The emphasis was very much centred on skills development and understanding the counselling process in terms of the theory, which was mainly psychodynamic. Counselling practice began at an early stage. In theory, this felt great, but as the time approached for my first session, I remember being gripped with anxiety. It felt like an exam and an interview rolled into one 50-minute ordeal. An old issue of 'doing it right' returned to haunt me.

The anxiety remained with me until I had got through the 'institutional' bits that are part of a first session when working in an agency (would I remember all the things I was supposed to?), then diminished as my focus shifted to 'being with the client' and to developing a rapport with the client. The first session went satisfactorily, and the client continued in counselling over a lengthy period. The training was the first time I really spent some time reflecting upon my identity in terms of my 'place' within an organization and among my peers as well as with clients. Interestingly, I never got the chance to work with anyone other than a white client during my time there, and clients did not seem to notice my 'difference' when such issues arose in the work. It was a different story with my peers. Some encouraged me to join the Black Workers' Support Group. I did so for a brief time, but found myself not 'fitting', so after some heartsearching I left the group. My experience of oppression, both personal and political, was quite different from the experiences of many people of African-Caribbean or Asian origin. Perhaps I was not 'black enough', and indeed have heard this implicitly in things said by both white and black people who would pressurize me to 'choose'. I felt strengthened in my position when I read the American cultural writer bell hooks (1991):

Teaching Black Studies, as I now do, I find that students are quick to label a black person who has grown up in a predominantly white setting and attended similar schools as 'not black enough.' I am shocked and annoyed where a white person explains to me that another black person is 'not black-identified.' Our concept of black experience has been too narrow and constricting. Rather than assume that a black person coming from a background that is not predominantly black is assimilationist, I prefer to acknowledge that theirs is a different black experience, one that means that they may not have had access to life experiences more common to those of us raised in a racially segregated worlds. It is not productive to see them as enemies or dismiss them by labelling them 'not black enough'. Most often, they have not chosen the context of their upbringing, and they may be suffering from a sense of 'loss' of not knowing who they are as black people or where they fit in.

During my time at the centre I decided to take a professional training in counselling, a postgraduate diploma. The orientation of the course was person-centred. I had decided to follow this direction as I had found myself increasingly at odds with the way that psychodynamic theory is sometimes seen by its practitioners as some sort of absolute truth, which when it does not 'work' is due to something about the client being 'unsuitable' for counselling or psychotherapy. My own experience in working with people who had been detained in special hospitals under the Mental Health Act convinced me of the value of therapeutic counselling. Rather than interpretation, I am most concerned with the actual relationship, as it is experienced, between counsellor and client. Reinforcement of my developing position was readily found in my reading, for example:

> The therapist encourages clients to experience themselves in relation to the therapist and to engage directly with their material rather than couch it in terms exclusively of their past or of their aspirations for the future (Mearns and Thorne, 1988).

And

> The distinctive feature about the person-centred approach is that it does not pay lip service to the importance of the relationship, but actually takes that as the aim of the counselling process with every client. In the person-centred approach, there is no withdrawal and retreat into exercises, interpretation or analysis of the client's behaviour (Mearns and Thorne, 1988).

I felt excited to be embarking on a new venture, and this overcame any anxiety I might have had at the prospect of starting a postgraduate course. Of the twenty-four students, there were only five men, one of whom was of Pakistani origin. After an introductory round of 'names' on the first day, we were invited to get into pairs and give a very potted life story. It was a good opportunity to be focused on us and to be very attentive to the other. Later in the day we took part in a guided fantasy of visualizing our names. I saw mine written in large black letters set against a bright white background. In my learning journal I wrote about how I was reminded of my 'mixed-raceness', and recalled a previous exercise when I had seen myself as a zebra! We then shared the history of our names with the group. It felt good to be encouraged to speak out loud of origins and background, to have them heard, and to feel valued. With hindsight, perhaps there was also some pleasure at feeling 'special' as well as different. I noticed that I was among the youngest of the students. I wondered when I would feel as 'grown-up' as the others seemed to be. I felt strange, and when we all began to talk to each other, I wonder if there was not a little element of competitiveness in our comparisons of our respective levels of experience (or grown-upness?), and how our paths had led us to this place.

One of the first things about the course that really impacted upon me, and on others, was the person-centredness of it all. It was both really challenging and really irritating! I had not experienced this style of education before, and was unused to having so much freedom to shape things. In fact I really hated sharing responsibility for the self-selection of tutorial groups. It felt like we were doing the tutorial staff's jobs. Why could they not have made it easier for us and sorted out the tutorial groups themselves? I have read since with more care the course handbook where it states that:

> The course philosophy acts as a paradigm, not only for the theoretical beliefs about persons within the counselling process, but also for our behaviour as course providers.

And that

> a further aspect of the centrality of respect for the person is the expectation that course members will take responsibility for their own learning and that the programme will have sufficient openness and flexibility to accommodate the implications of negotiating with adult learners. Staff

members are not expected to deny their expertise, and for this reason there is a considerable part of each course designated as core studies; but ... in the Diploma course, there are negotiable areas of the curriculum and areas of the assessment system that can be tailored to the course members' needs and interests on the basis of negotiation.

Having said that, there was a basic structure for the term given to us, and it indicated the core elements of the course: the written work, and how we could negotiate the form a significant part of it could take; the tutor groups; skills practice; group process time when the whole group came together at the beginning and ending of each day; supervision groups with a strong formative and tutor led element.

Although some parts of the handbook were not fully digested in advance, I do remember being impressed by the commitment shown to the 'social context of counselling', an area of central importance to any kind of 'people work', and to counselling and psychotherapy training in particular. In particular,

> Research into counselling and training for counsellors and supervisors has begun to make clear that the training and development of counsellors (like that of many other professional groups) has frequently failed to make an adequate exploration of the oppressive nature of the society in which it operates. In consequence it has relied on highly individualised models of persons and of their troubles, which can lead to unhelpful approaches to many who are in need of help, and the development of services which are not equally accessible or useful to all who might need them. The broad 'liberal' perspective that has characterised such education and training may, at worst, lead to the further oppression of those that counselling seeks to help. Counsellors seeing the difficulties their clients encounter as wholly personal issues about which they have complete freedom of choice, and understanding their difficulties in using counselling as 'resistance' rather than an expression of different cultural norms or values, perceive every failure of the counselling process as due to the client's failings rather than to their own internalised oppressive structures.

Looking back through my learning journal, I see that the subject of my identity in terms of colour came up frequently in pairs exercises and in my relationship to the large group. Although in the large group I did not speak out as much as I could have, or would do now, I know that I wavered between a sense of pride in my uniqueness and a feeling that it would be so much easier if I was just like 'them'.

Various 'cluster' exercises formed a significant part of the beginning of the course. During these exercises I often felt alienated, manipulated and quite at sea. At times I felt confused, angry, and feared rejection. I found myself resisting an urge to 'fit in' or to belong to something I did not yet know, perhaps by wanting to take charge of some of the exercises in order to reduce my anxiety. Some of these initial exercises involved making uninformed choices. This still does not make much sense to me. Only if I (metaphorically) squint very hard can I see that it might have been about taking one's own responsibility for choices and that we have a part to play in shaping whatever community we 'belong' to. I do remember and continue to value a comment made to me at this time by one of the course team; he wondered if I had thought that everything about the course should be 'comfortable', and that perhaps this was a time to challenge this.

A question of identity

The course soon encountered a crisis when the person who was due to teach the social context component of the course withdrew at a very late stage, which meant that another workshop provider stepped in at short notice. The first workshop of the module was supposed to deal with issues of oppression and (in)equality. I felt and continue to feel that it was a huge disappointment and a waste of an opportunity. It was almost completely experiential and the task of the small group to which I belonged was to present our case as a displaced 'Black African Muslim Minority Tribe' to the leaders of a country where we would like to have settled. As I write this, I find myself again becoming angry that no attention was paid to the complexities of the structural racism that pervades white Britain, let alone the racism that exists between non-white communities. During the workshop I attempted to begin to discuss this, but was told in no uncertain terms by the workshop leader that 'only white people can be racist'. End of discussion! I can afford myself a wry smile when I recall that the same workshop leader made a comment to the fact that all bar one of the participants were white . . . well I remember the Asian trainee being there as well as me'! Once more I experienced alienation as the very person who was supposed to be teaching the group about racism and oppression was ignoring my colour. This was despite having earlier had an introductory 'names' round, which might have suggested to her that my origins are something other than white. While I am mindful of the fact that we all develop our awareness of these issues at different rates, and that even then we will probably not all agree, I think that this course should have really grasped this opportunity for some real discourse at this early stage. Instead the workshop was an exercise in political correctness devoid of any depth, analysis of the social context, and did not offer any critique of how racism and oppression can be understood. I feel it is fortunate and am glad that both the course community and core teaching staff took responsibility and made time to discuss some of the problems that were widely acknowledged to have arisen out of this workshop, some of which were subsequently addressed. We also had opportunities in various workshops to explore issues such as working transculturally, social/structural inequality, disability, gender and sexuality. These issues remained 'alive' and were frequently discussed during the course. In contrast to my experience on the previous course, I like to think that this was in part due to the person-centredness of the diploma course. As a course community, with the encouragement of the course leaders, we were able to shape some of the inputs to better meet our learning objectives.

I had been looking forward to getting to grips with the academic side of the course both as a personal intellectual challenge and because I felt, and still feel, that a professional counselling training should have a rigorous academic component to it. One of the greatest challenges to be met was the negotiation with my tutor of an 'assessed portfolio' of work which was to form about thirty per cent of the total work to be presented (the equivalent of about 25,000 words). To enable us to do this, we were provided with a list of the eleven syllabus elements of the course and given clear guidelines as to which form of assessment might be used for each syllabus area. 'Forms of assessment' were essays; case studies; video and audio recordings of counselling sessions; project work; and presentations. The negotiated element of the assessed work was, I thought, a really creative way of enabling all course participants to find the best way for them to meet their learning objectives. It seems to me that counsellor-training courses, which insist on their students completing a lengthy dissertation, lose more than they gain by not allowing all their students an equal chance to flourish and demonstrate their competence as practitioners. After all, not everyone comes to train as a counsellor by way of traditional academic routes that may have long essay writing as the norm.

Essays presented no special difficulties over and above any I had faced during my psychology degree. It was a question of choosing a subject that fitted into the (quite complicated) guidelines we were given. Likewise, other pieces of written work came relatively easily to me. I was most concerned about the assessed video and audio recordings of practice. I felt so exposed, and wondered if they would find out that I was the most incompetent counsellor in the whole city, if not the world! I was reassured that most of my peers felt the same as I did. I had to get used to having microphones and cameras around and to overcome my anxiety to be seen to be 'doing' counselling properly. What if I forgot how to do it? I felt some expectations that I should be good at it as I already had some experience as a counsellor. The feelings were somewhat reminiscent of those I encountered as a child when the possibility of having to be in a school play arose. In those circumstances I would choose to be a 'tree' or a member of a crowd and thus avoid the problems of getting my lines wrong. But there was no hiding place now. Eventually, as the course progressed I largely overcame this fear, although I feel that being oneself in the counselling room, being 'congruent', 'genuine' or whatever you want to call it, is both the simplest yet most sophisticated and difficult of Rogers' core conditions for a beginning person-centred counsellor (Rogers, 1961). I was no exception in finding this exceptionally problematic. Rogers said that

> If therapy is to occur, it seems necessary that the therapist be, in the relationship, a unified, or integrated, or congruent person. What I mean is that within the relationship he is exactly what he is − not a facade, or a role, or a pretense (*sic*) . . . it is when the therapist is fully and accurately aware of what he is experiencing at this moment in the relationship, that he is fully congruent.

I think that at first I attributed my difficulty with congruence to the fact that it did not fit in with my previous psychodynamic training. In reality I think this was a convenient intellectual hiding place, and that really I was afraid, and did not know how to 'do' it.

The course settled quickly into a pattern of group time at either end of the day sandwiching skills development sessions; tutorial time; theory input; time for peer assessment of each others' work (something completely new to me that I found very rewarding to do); and workshops covering the various syllabus areas I mentioned earlier. The subject of assessing my peers' work involved paying very close attention to detail and strict criteria. The most interesting area of peer assessment was of counselling skills demonstrations where we were to look for the presence and communication of the core conditions using scales devised by Carkhuff (1969). Until I had seen these scales, I had not really thought about how counselling can be deconstructed in such a way.

This pattern largely continued in the second year when we also started to spend some time on our 'alternative theory' module. I regret now that I chose psychodynamic theory, as I was aware that I had significantly moved away from that position, and would perhaps gain relatively little from investigating further at that stage. However, I am ashamed to say it was the easy option as I already had done a lot of the required reading. On second thoughts as I consider this statement, I would prefer to call it a 'pragmatic option', given that I was still in full-time employment as a residential social worker, with two sleep-ins a week, as well as being a volunteer counsellor. I do not think I could have realistically spared the time and energy on learning about something wholly new. I feel I am now making up for this lost opportunity in that I am beginning to explore the existential-phenomenological approach with a view to further training.

With hindsight, I was disappointed that the course did not pay attention to concepts of mental health/illness. While I understand that the person-centred approach is instinctively against this framework, I think it was foolish not to include grounding in theories of mental health, whether or not we agree with them. After all, in the world 'out there' many counsellors work alongside health professionals whose frame of reference is based in the medical/psychiatric model. I feel it is important at least to be able to use a common language, thus facilitating communication and understanding between disciplines. My view is that without the training and/or experience to assess for serious mental health difficulties, a counsellor may put the client, the community and him/herself at risk. If these issues are not given attention during a 'professional counselling training', then I have to wonder where the counsellor is expected to acquire such learning. I have only recently formed a strong opinion on this, and I guess that when I was training I took my own knowledge and experience of working with people with mental health problems for granted. Since then I have become very concerned when I have met and talked with counsellors with no training or experience in this area, who have felt quite at sea when they come across disturbed clients. While I do not favour a 'diagnostic' approach to counselling and psychotherapy, I do think that we can all be informed by psychiatry without accepting all that it says as some sort of unassailable and absolute truth. A workshop given by the psychiatrist Dr Suman Fernando at the very end of the course made so much sense to me both on a personal and a professional level. He presented the issues raised in his book *Mental Health, Race & Culture* (Fernando, 1991) and he talked about the fact that many psychiatric diagnoses are culturally mediated rather than based on any absolute truth. I felt both supported and challenged by his thinking, and I realized that despite of my own deeply held beliefs about people, and despite my best intentions, I could quite easily slip both into prejudices and the reassuring certainties of the Western medical model. I do not wish to suggest that I reject this model, as I feel it has a great deal of validity in many situations and that it can be a valuable tool in our understanding of human beings. However, I cannot envisage it being at the centre of my practice as a counsellor. I would encourage a stance which enables the maintenance of a critical distance from anything which claims to be *the truth* (whatever that is); a stance which permits a scientific scepticism, and which does not lose sight of the uniqueness and potential of each therapeutic relationship. This workshop could have been a platform for the course to embark on a greater exploration of psychiatric diagnoses, mental health in general and its interface with the field of counselling and psychotherapy. Unfortunately, as I said earlier, it was not to be.

Who am I?

Towards the end of the first year the issue of racism, and a group member's experience of being on the receiving end of it, manifested itself within the group, particularly during course community time at the beginning and end of the day. It ended up with the group being traumatized and splitting into, with hindsight, predictable camps. There were those who said nothing; those who sat resolutely on the fence who felt there must have been a misunderstanding; the diehard anti-racists who were for 'doing something'; and me. I did not know where to stand at first, as I seemed to be able to see all sides of the argument. I sensed my own resistance to being swept along by the strong feelings present in the group. For reasons of confidentiality

I cannot elaborate on the circumstances to which I refer. However, I would say that my own personal learning from this was incredibly painful with respect to the dilemmas I experienced as to how I identified myself in terms of colour and to whom my allegiances ultimately lay in this case. It felt like I would be betraying the only other person of colour in the group if I were not to side with him. I felt myself moving towards more fully embracing myself as a person of mixed-race in a culture where racism is pervasive. I learned more from this experience than in most of the 'social context' workshops put together. I cannot emphasize enough how important I think it is for community time (or whatever it may be called) to be built in to counsellor training courses. Even if it can sometimes seem like the most tedious or painful thing on earth! I was by now making a choice to move away from the 'black or white' argument, with its polarized positions, and began to identify myself as a person of colour (a term which is used far more in North America than in the United Kingdom). At present I feel at home in this place I have made for myself, and feel it reflects my heritage better. I do not think I would have made this shift so soon without my reflections in personal therapy and elsewhere, and my experiences on the course. Incidentally, I have since found that I have something in common with people who identify themselves as bisexual, in that there is this sense of being pressurized to 'choose' between what are opposite positions that do not describe who we are.

The effects of my self-identification as a person of colour have had repercussions in my counselling with clients. Now that I can see myself more clearly, I feel I am better able to see clients as they are, and more than that, the relationship that is created between us feels fuller in the sense that I am more aware of who I am bringing to it.

Picking up the gauntlet

As the course was entering its final months I decided, with the support of my partner, to take a major risk: to pick up the gauntlet I had thrown down to myself several years before. I felt ready to try to earn my living as a counsellor and decided that I preferred this not to be in independent practice. So, with no jobs being advertised, I set about enquiring about the possibility of working in the National Health Service (NHS). I made contact with a local NHS rehabilitation centre for people who are receiving treatment for various physical injuries, head/brain injuries, or who require pain management. My decision to do this was informed partly by my own treatment there following a near fatal accident a few months before I commenced my training, and partly because, by chance, I had counselled ex-patients of the unit who felt their emotional and psychological needs had not been sufficiently met during their treatment. I put forward my ideas and asked the management if they could employ me on a sessional basis for a trial period. After agreeing to my proposals I was invited to meet with the entire staff group. Their responses ranged from scepticism to enthusiasm, the latter winning out. I think it was a question of being in the right place at the right time, as the centre's philosophy was becoming more holistic and they had a little spare money as the result of an unfilled post. Procedures for referral were agreed, issues of privacy and confidentiality were discussed and my hourly rates established. The experiment has been a success as I remain there to this day, three years later. However, I am now officially employed as a part-time counsellor, and in addition to individual work I run a group as part of the pain management programme.

At about the same time I started working one afternoon a week in a local hospital's department of clinical genetics. There, I see patients who have been assessed by the medical team as needing therapeutic input over and above that which is provided by the genetic nurse specialists/genetic counsellors. It is mainly through my experiences in the NHS in these areas of work that I have come to want to more fully explore the existential approach, as it seems to me to best describe the work I do. Every day I find myself working with people whose 'way of being-in-the-world' has become shaken by, for example, an injury that has left them with a disability; or by a diagnosis of some genetic condition which may have profound effects on their sense of what life means to them, or suddenly being faced with the certainty that their children's lives will not turn out as they had hoped, or perhaps being faced with the feelings of loss for their children now never to be born. I meet people whose assumptions about their physical being and their sense of themselves in relation to others has been transformed. Their 'sedimentations', or to put it another way, their values and behaviour patterns, are very much at odds with how they now experience themselves. In many of these cases the people I encounter are beset with death anxiety or as

Spinelli (1997) calls it, 'temporal life anxiety'. To quote Emmy van Deurzen-Smith (1987):

> The aim of existential counselling is to clarify, reflect upon and understand life. Problems in living are confronted and life's possibilities and boundaries are explored. Existential counselling does not set out to cure people in the tradition of the medical model. Clients are considered to be not ill but sick of life or clumsy at living. When people are confused and lost the last thing they need is to be treated as ill or incompetent. What they need is some assistance in surveying the terrain and in deciding on the right route so that they can again find their way.

As the course drew to a close and my assignments had been completed, my focus began to shift elsewhere and I longed for it to end. Looking back at my notes, I find them much sparser than they had been for the previous 18 months. I was putting a lot of energy into the paid practice. My energies were redirected into establishing both myself as a counsellor and the profession of counselling in contexts where it had previously not existed. The course ended with an 'away day' – an opportunity to say what we needed to say to each other and to bid each other farewell.

Important lessons

The two years of the course were, I feel, overall, a great learning experience, both personally and academically. Without it, I would not now have the opportunities I have to practise as a counsellor. It was not perfect by any means, but I wonder how challenging a 'perfect course', if it could ever exist, would be without the struggles we had to endure. It is impossible to summarize all I learned during the training, but I feel that I can crystallize some of the most important lessons:

- Carl Rogers' core conditions are the bedrock of my work as a counsellor.
- There is no substitute for learning in a group. I cannot conceive of training as a counsellor by distance learning.
- Counselling is not about 'curing'; it is about being in a process of enabling a more authentic way of living, to become open to our existence.

- There is no escape from the paradox of being 'alone' in our experience while 'being with others'.
- I cannot presume to 'know' what a client experiences, I can only have a sense of it by doing my best to get alongside them.
- That I am responsible for my actions.

Since I completed this phase of training I have become accredited by the BAC, and am now an accreditation assessor. I have left my social work job and now practise full-time as a counsellor, dividing my time more or less equally between my work in the NHS, and a half-time university post.

References

Carkhuff, R. (1969) *Helping and human relations*, New York: Holt, Rinehart & Winston

Fernando, S. (1991) Mental Health, Race and Culture, London: Macmillan.

hooks, b. (1991) *Yearning: Race, gender, and cultural politics*, London: Turnaround.

Mearns, D. and Thorne, B. (1988) *Person-Centred Counselling in Action*, London: Sage.

Spinelli, E. (1997) *Tales of Un-knowing. Therapeutic encounters from an existential perspective*, London: Duckworth.

Rogers, C. (1961) *On Becoming a Person. A therapist's view of psychotherapy*, Boston: Houghton Mifflin.

van Deurzen-Smith, E. (1988) *Existential Counselling in Practice*, London: Sage.

3

The Consequences of Clarity

Hylda Taylor-Smith

When Hylda Taylor-Smith set out to increase her counselling competencies in order to enhance her effectiveness as a co-ordinator of a youth counselling project, little did she anticipate the psychological impact that her training course would have upon her. She recounts how issues that she had pushed to the back of her mind increasingly came to the foreground and demanded immediate addressing. Thus, she examines issues such as racism, power, inequality, vulnerability, oppression, prejudice and the problems of cross-cultural counselling. Zones of potential conflict are identified and the case for quality supervision is strongly argued.

In 1993 I was appointed co-ordinator of a pilot project introduced by a local authority youth service. The project was to set up and run an information and counselling centre aimed at young people of ages 14–25. Although I had experience of youth work and management, I had only a basic training and experience of counselling. It soon became clear to me that I needed to undergo further training in counselling in order to fulfil the remit of my job. This view was only grudgingly accepted by my then line manager. Over the period of my development as a counsellor our differing views about what was required in providing a counselling service became further sharply divided.

I spent a considerable amount of time weighing up what I needed to get from any counselling course that I decided to undertake. I was determined to only commit myself to a course that demonstrated a clear understanding and grasp of issues around counselling, race, oppression and cultural difference. I felt very strongly that as a black mature student I was not going to submit to the tokenism and casual white racism that I had experienced in other educational settings. I believed that counselling, as a professional field that was relatively new, should be addressing the issues that are very much a part of living in a multicultural society. I was very excited when I read the prospectus for the course I eventually followed and felt after my interview with the course leader that there was a genuine commitment to taking on the challenges posed by the issues around race and cultural difference within the course and its approach.

Having been accepted onto the course, major changes in my personal circumstances occurred in the intervening year. By the time I was due to take up my place on the course, I was pregnant with my third child. I made the decision to delay for another year. So by the time I became a trainee counsellor, my baby daughter was eight months old and I had only just returned to full-time employment after six months maternity leave. I found the return to work and the first three months of the course very stressful. The stresses were in part due to the sheer logistics of working full-time, studying part-time and coping with a young baby. The added difficulty of travelling an 80-miles round trip to the training institution each week and organizing childcare proved fraught at times.

Some of the stresses were related to the enormity of the task that I had undertaken – the task of becoming a counsellor. I felt very unconfident and inadequate regarding my abilities. I was daunted by the intellectual challenge of acquiring new understandings of ways of looking at the world and people. It also became clear that I was going to be challenged through my exposure and contact with the course members and tutors, in relation to my own values and beliefs and prejudices. The process of getting to know people on the course and opening myself up to the possibility of acceptance and/or rejection by them meant that the first few months of the course were particularly fraught. From the beginning, I derived an enormous amount of comfort and a sense of security from the presence on the course of two other African-Caribbean women and two Indian women.

A new agenda

When I started training, I believed that I was entering a new phase of my personal and professional development. I felt secure in terms of my personal life and reasonably confident professionally. I had made a strong case for my need to train as a counsellor in order to fulfil the requirements of my job and that case had been accepted. My employer agreed to pay for half of the course fees and allowed me the time off each week to attend the course. So while I was aware that the physical demands over the next two years would be taxing, I felt up to the challenge. However, I was not prepared for the psychological demands of the changes that occurred in me, as a consequence of doing the course. What I had not bargained for were the consequences of clarity.

Maybe I should try to explain what I mean by that. Attending the course each week opened up a space for self-analysis, reflection and challenge that I found at times relentless. Issues in my life that had quietly been put on the back-burner started to move onto my agenda of issues that needed addressing. After a while they started to move up the agenda in terms of priority. It was not that this process was forced upon me, far from it. It was a consequence of struggling to understand myself and my motives better in the belief that so doing would enable me to empathize with clients. In committing myself to a person-centred approach, openness and honesty with myself became a prerequisite of every activity. While on the course I learned to admit to myself that I was often not honest and open, the standards that I set for myself made such knowledge increasingly hard to bear.

So, fairly rapidly the confidence that had enabled me to embark on training started to break down. What replaced it was anxiety about my ability to successfully complete the course and doubts as to whether I was a suitable person to become a counsellor. I felt that the language and concepts of counselling were elusive and obscure. I felt that in order to become a counsellor I might be required to change into someone that I would not be able to recognize. I feared that I might just not be good enough. This was not false humility on my part; I had been offering counselling and support to young people as part of my job for a number of years. I thought that I had understood what was meant by those terms. My training, however, made it clear that what I had been offering was very limited. It was also confused, particularly in relation to boundaries. I felt that the youth service accepted a blurring of boundaries when issues were raised about the distinction between, on the one hand, a youth worker offering emotional support to a young person, as, on the other, negotiating a counselling relationship between a young person and a worker. I became more and more uneasy that such a set up left both youth workers and young people, in a grey area where they were both at risk of emotional abuse. It was neither ethically nor professionally satisfactory.

Being black – becoming a counsellor

I have always been black but I have only recently begun to think of myself as a counsellor. It is true to say that my awareness of my racial identity emerged gradually throughout my childhood. Yet I have thought of myself as black from around the age of five. Although my thoughts about my blackness might shift and change with the development of my political and spiritual awareness, being black and my consciousness of it is part of my identity and my understanding of myself. It is not the sum total of who I am but it is an integral part of what it means to be me.

Becoming a counsellor was a potential challenge to my understanding of how I saw myself. I was fearful that becoming a counsellor might conflict with my blackness. I needed assurance that becoming a counsellor would expand what it meant to be me – that I would experience a welcoming of diversity from the course community. But it seemed that the behaviour of the tutors and the students changed whenever the black students raised issues around race and cultural difference. I believe that their personal fears and anxieties around issues of race negatively affected their responses in discussions. The course curriculum addressed some of the issues of racial and cultural difference in the social context element of the course. While I found this valuable, discussions were focused, narrowly in my view, within a sociological framework. What I felt was missing was an informed discussion about practice, supervision and professionalism by counsellors in training, led by the course tutors, regarding issues or race and cultural difference. It was left to individuals within the course group as a whole or in smaller informal groups to deal with any issues when they were raised outside of the social context focus on race. Along with several other black students (as well as some of the white students), I felt that this approach did not take into account the fears and anxieties that might result in people feeling unable to address uncomfortable emotions. Often, it seemed that the vast majority of the course group preferred to leave well alone and there was a conspicuous silence when racial issues were raised. At other times, issues were raised as a matter of anger and frustration that they were being ducked. Each time the course group struggled to acknowledge racism, cultural difference and the concept of a black perspective in counselling, it seemed to me that the black students became targets of some of the fear, anxiety, suspicion and hostility within the group. I felt that issues of race were deemed to be of too narrow an interest compared to the wider concerns of counselling and a person-centred approach. I felt, and still do, that these issues pose serious challenges to the practice of counsellors, but they are not adequately addressed in training. My experience of training has clarified these issues for me, and they are:

- An individual's need to be seen and understood includes the acceptance of their racial and cultural identity, as defined by themselves. Are counsellors being equipped to explore these areas within their training?
- The psychological and emotional impact on the therapeutic alliance of issues around power, inequality, vulnerability and oppression.
- An exploration of prejudice and fear of difference linked with considerations of counsellor practice is an issue to be raised in personal therapy.

Developing practice

I worked as a trainee counsellor for one half day a week for just over one year at a university student counselling service. The placement provided me with the opportunity to engage in a practical way with clients and try to address some of the concerns that they brought; and, at the same time, the opportunity to use the framework for practice offered by a person-centred approach to counselling. For quite a long time I felt completely inadequate to the task; I felt overwhelmed by the range and depth of distress that my clients chose to share with me. Only very gradually over the months did I gain the insight that in order to be genuine with my clients, I had to be comfortable enough with who I was and 'let go' concerns related to my ego to be accepting of myself in order to focus on my clients – concerns such as, do I look right?, do I sound right? It sounds such a simple thing and yet I initially found it difficult to put into practice. One of the reasons for this, I believe, was connected with my being black and most of my clients being white. As a black counsellor and a trainee, I initially felt heightened anxiety about the possibility of being rejected by potential clients once they realized that their counsellor was to be a black woman. I did indeed encounter one client whose response when I met him in the counselling service reception for our first meeting was distinctly hostile. The ensuing 50 minutes that we spent in each other's company was among the most uncomfortable that I have ever experienced. Ironically, my client's presenting problem was that people did not seem to like him and that he felt alienated from them; increasingly this was creating problems for him because he had no friends and was dubious that he would be able to secure a job. I tried to explore with him whether he was willing to commit himself to a process that would involve focusing on how he reacts and interacts with the world. He was looking, he said, for guidance in terms of techniques that might help him present himself more successfully. I was aware of a wariness about our discussion and lack of psychological contact. It came as no surprise when he decided not to commit himself to counselling with me.

I will never know whether my client's negative response to me was a result of my colour or part of the general difficulty that he had identified that he had in dealing with people. What I learned from meeting him was that I allowed my preoccupation with his initially negative response to me to get in the way and this made it difficult for me to be real. To be real I would have had to summon up the courage to share my disquiet at his initial response to me and to feed back my perception of hostility on his part. I am saying all this with hindsight; I still may not have made psychological contact but my being real with him could have acted as a release that would have allowed him to be real with me.

Early on during my placement I found that the first meeting with a client would inevitably cause me to feel extremely anxious. I realized that my anxiety was rooted in a fear of being rejected. Eventually I found that as I grew in confidence and self-awareness that my anxiety lessened. I learned to channel my energies into being more calm and relaxed and encouraging my clients to express their anxieties rather than let them become overwhelming – which is when they can take on a life of their own.

Confusion: being guided by the client

A central feature of a person-centred approach to counselling is that it is the client who has both the knowledge of what is causing their distress and what they want to do about it. It seems to me that a person-centred counsellor provides a safe, non-judgemental, caring environment and facilitates the client's self-discovery about what their root concern is, what is at the heart of their soul's disquiet, and what, if any, action they would like to take in resolving it (if it can be resolved).

During the first few months of working as a trainee counsellor, one of the issues that I struggled with was confusion, both my own and the client's. The combined demands of the course, my job and caring for a child not yet one year old, meant that I often became overwhelmed by my different priorities and responsibilities. Sometimes I felt myself sinking into a state of confusion and turmoil while at the same time attempting to work with clients also facing some form of crisis in their life. There was a particular client, a young man whom I shall call Joe, who was facing a range of dilemmas in terms of his financial affairs, his relationships and his coursework. He actually apologized to me for being confused and for being unsure about what to do. I found myself saying to him that it was okay to be confused and it felt as though I was giving myself permission to be confused as well as being accepting of my client's confusion. It seemed to me that Joe had possibly feared that his feelings of panic and his situation might be reinforced by me. I think he might also have picked up that chaos and confusion were states that I found very uncomfortable to be in for any length of time. Since my work at the time involved a substantial amount of advice giving to young people, the temptation that I often faced was to resort to a problem-solving mindset, as a way of bypassing painful, uncomfortable feelings. What I discovered through my work with Joe is that confusion signifies a need for change and that confusion, while uncomfortable, can be a motivating force and can release creativity. This was a valuable lesson that I reminded myself of constantly during the two years of the course.

Dynamics in the group

The initial course group consisted of 24 people, including two Indian women, three Jamaican women and three white men. The course community was therefore predominantly white and female. The course leader was white and male and the second course tutor was white and female.

From the beginning, I experienced a sense of unease and tension within the white course members when discussing issues regarding race, cultural difference and racism. I felt that this uneasiness often got in the way of establishing a friendly relationship between black and white course members. I also felt that the course tutors were uncertain in their handling of issues relating to the possible and actual tensions that can exist between individuals of different cultures. It felt to me that we were part of a dynamic that inevitably reflected some of the issues that we were asked to address as an academic concern. Yet when black course members tried to articulate their need for the topics of race, racism, and cultural diversity in a counselling context to be discussed, the whole group seemed to succumb to a form of collective dumbness. I often felt that silence was being used as a defence and as a weapon. So for at least the first year and well into the second year, it seemed that there was an uneasy unspoken understanding that the subject of relationships between black and white people was too frightening to talk about in any depth. I was disappointed and frustrated that a group of people committed to openness and honesty were not able to find ways of exploring these fears together. This indicated a lack of trust, which in turn made it difficult for me to trust course members and tutors in respect of other issues. I do believe that learning institutions need to treat black students in a way that allows them to feel safe and so able to learn.

By the end of the course, however, we had as a course group managed to move away from the place of fear and defensiveness regarding the racial issues around. The change came about partly as a result of people beginning to feel more confident about themselves and grounded in who they are. Also the persistence of a number of students (both black and white) in raising their concerns resulted in a black practitioner being invited to lead a day workshop addressing some of the issues. Notwithstanding the progress made, I still feel that the course tutors could have offered more in terms of engaging the course community in discussing how racism might impact upon their professional practice.

The impact of training on my job

I had worked within the context of a youth service for several years, managing a centre providing educational and leisure facilities for young black adults. During this time I became interested in developing my interpersonal skills and did some basic level counselling training. When the opportunity came up to develop the advice and counselling service for young people, I was really excited. For several years, the project consisted of a part-time administrator and myself; we did not have premises or any staff to work with. When staff were appointed they consisted of two qualified youth workers and a trained librarian. Although staff had wide experience of using counselling skills and providing young people with support and advice, I was the only one with a specific (and basic) qualification in counselling. None of us had worked for a counselling service before. I felt that in order for the project to progress in relation to its counselling remit, there needed to be at least one member of staff who was a trained counsellor. This view was not readily accepted by my then manager and after agreeing to fund one year of my training, she attempted to renege on that agreement a fortnight before the course was due to start. The situation was only resolved when I appealed to her line manager.

I was excited and optimistic about the prospect of the training because I felt that not only was I going to benefit from it, personally and professionally, but that I could pass on my learning to my staff team who had supported the case for a trained counsellor. Unfortunately, the requirements of the course meant that I was away from the project two days a week. I was aware that often the staff team were overstretched by my absence and although we had all agreed that in the long term the project would benefit from my training, I felt guilty. However, as I became more involved in the course and what I was learning, I became more aware that the project that I had embarked upon in such a spirit of optimism and naiveté was, in fact, deeply flawed. I began to realize that if a project describes itself as a counselling service, it has certain ethical and moral responsibilities and these had not been considered. One of the most basic requirements was counselling supervision for workers engaged in offering counselling whether they were trained counsellors or not. I began to realize the difference between counselling supervision and managerial supervision. I was giving my staff managerial supervision but they were identifying the need for counselling supervision. Since I was in the process of becoming a counsellor and receiving counselling supervision for the first time, I was not the appropriate person. There were very few people within the service with sufficient experience of counselling supervision to offer it in-house. Therefore, yet again, I was asking for additional resources from my manager to support those members of staff who were counselling young people. In the meanwhile, the demand for counselling among young people started to increase. The project was moving towards a crisis.

Another issue that proved problematic was confidentiality. Since the local education authority funded my project, the procedures regarding confidentiality, particularly in relation to child abuse, sexual or otherwise, were quite rigid. A young person, particularly under the age of 16, who disclosed sexual abuse, could quite rapidly find themselves taken over by the machinery of the local authority's responsibilities under the Children's Act 1989. A person-centred counsellor working in this context is faced with holding quite contradictory priorities. On the one hand, there is the trust of a young person that you will respect her/his autonomy and rights; and on the other hand, there are the legitimate concerns expressed through legislation that action is taken to investigate and where evidence is found to prosecute perpetrators of child abuse. What can often happen is that the emotions of the young person and their need to feel strong enough and good enough becomes secondary to the demand that a procedure is followed whose primary concern is that action is seen to be taken. In order for action to be seen to be taken, more people need to be informed of the facts – confidentiality has to be broken to remain professional as a youth worker, and yet to breach confidentiality is to bring into disrepute the very thing which underpins a positive relationship, namely trust. Since I was the manager of the project and responsible for supervising other staff, these dilemmas were a constant preoccupation to me. The more I developed my skills and confidence as a counsellor in training, the harder it became to attempt to rationalize the contradictions that I faced.

Turning point

Eventually something had to give. I wanted to accept the clarity and guidance offered by working within the framework offered by the British Association of Counselling (BAC) code of practice, but the youth service could not wholly take on the BAC code of practice. I felt that I was constantly falling down the gap that existed between two different cultures, which were similar on the surface but radically different in principle and practice.

Three months before completing my diploma, I decided that I was a counsellor not a youth worker. While I was trying to be both a youth worker and a counsellor, I was in a constant state of anxiety and unease. I was not doing justice to either role. By January 1997 I had reached a turning point. My dissatisfaction with the job, coupled with anxiety over the health of a seriously ill relative and the demands of the course, left me in a state of turmoil. During a practice training session (which was being filmed, and I was in the role of client and a fellow student was in the role of counsellor), I shared my frustration and finally voiced aloud what I had previously felt but not expressed – I could not continue to do that job. As I expressed the feeling and acknowledged it to be true, everything else fell into place. I resigned my post. Once I had made my decision and acted upon it, the turmoil ceased and I felt real again.

Despite the difficulties that resulted from giving up a well-paid job, I have never regretted it. In order to become the kind of counsellor I aspired to be, I first had to give up something. That something was the illusion that if I tried to do my best, then somehow that would make up for the ethical compromises, blurring of boundaries, contradictions and lack of clarity that bedevilled the service I worked for.

Conclusion and lessons learned

This chapter consists of two quite distinct narratives: one concerned with my reflections on how my blackness and sense of identity impacted upon my experience of training; the other with my professional development as a youth worker, the original motivation to undergo counsellor training. From the entwined experience of these two narratives, I have learned some key lessons about myself and about counselling:

• The training is a catalyst and acts as a compass but it is just part of a much longer journey.
• I learned that personal development and growth is to be welcomed, I also learned that change is both painful and causes pain.

- I learned to value the people in my life who did not feel threatened by the changes in me and chose to become involved in my development.
- I learned an enormous amount in terms of factual information but I also learned about relationships and emotions by being with people who dared to express them and share them. It is this that makes me fully appreciate the courage of clients who expose their heart and pain to me.
- I learned to be more trusting and less rigid.
  I learned that the process of growth is ongoing and that the opportunities are always there for it to happen, if we open ourselves up to it and overcome our fears.

I am still surprised that the effect of my training was a re-evaluation of my job and the decision to leave it, whereas my initial concerns about training were anticipated difficulties regarding the treatment of race and culture on the course and my need to defend my blackness. Ironically, these were not the issues that provoked a sense of crisis for me. The crisis I ultimately faced was one of professional integrity and clarity.

4

I Never Thought Empathy Would Be So Difficult

Joan Rogers

Having reached the 'top of the tree' in one profession, deciding to make a fundamental career change in early middle age is as unnerving as it is challenging. Joan Rogers gives a vivid picture of what it means to open up to one's own vulnerability and woundedness and to value oneself. This, she argues, is the best gift that a training course can give and, consequentially, what a counsellor can give to the client. It is the person of the counsellor that facilitates the therapeutic process, more so than the techniques or the skills employed. Doing 'weird things' in the course of learning to respect oneself and others involves pain, rewards – and fun.

My name is Joan Rogers, and at the time of writing I am 44-years-old, divorced with two boys of eleven- and eight-years-old: one is musical, the other a football fanatic, and I love them to pieces. I work as chief executive of an NHS Trust that includes hospital, community and mental health services; and I work in a counselling clinic once a week in another NHS Trust.

As I begin to write this chapter, I am imagining a reader who is considering undertaking counsellor training, as I was in 1995. I have worried about how to start to describe three years of counsellor training. In writing the chapter, I have found out certain things about myself. What I have learned is not rocket science, but I have found that for me it has been difficult to write about counsellor training in the singular. Instead what I have written has echoed, recalled, and exemplified other relationships, and most especially, the counselling relationship. Many of these echoes reverberate and call up other meanings beyond the experience of training. Thus this chapter will try to be concrete, real, and I hope helpful to the reader, without being mysterious.

I begin by saying that the training gained in richness and meaning across a period of three years, starting with a certificate course followed by a two year diploma course. At any particular point in time, the meanings held then cast back over, and changed or enhanced what had gone before. I now understand this to be something like the nature of hermeneutic research, as I work towards an MA by completing a research thesis!

This widening and deepening of earlier experience as the training progressed may owe something to the philosophy of the course. In the introductory course material there was a long and very beautiful poem. It is called *Ithaka*, and is by C. P. Cavafy (1961). It takes the form of a description of a journey to the island of Ithaka in the Ionian Sea and what may be gained on the way and what may be found, or not found, at journey's end. It is full of allusion and metaphor and it ends as follows:

> And if you find her poor, Ithaka won't have fooled you,
> Wise as you will have become, so full of experience,
> You'll have understood by then what these Ithakas mean.

Well, I thought I understood it then, when I received it, although I think I may have been a bit dubious about course instructions that also sent me a poem! I can remember going for interview and seeing through a window three women hugging each other! Maybe I thought *Ithaka* was more of the same!

When I read it now, it moves me deeply, although I think I am only beginning to understand it. It throws light on my journey as a trainee, and it illuminates something about the course philosophy, and the tutors who wanted this poem to be part of the instructions for joining the course. It feels as if they were trying to reach out and tell us something, something really important. Yet paradoxically it was something that perhaps could not be fully understood, at the start of the journey. I see this chapter as my prose version of *Ithaka*. It does have, and will have meaning, although the reader may need to come round again to 'see' it all.

Tensions in training

A theme in this chapter, therefore, is tension and paradox. It is about the tension I have felt while writing the chapter, the tension between my wish to impart knowledge of counsellor training, the stuff', the facts, and my sense that I am giving myself. And when I am giving myself it feels as if the facts about counsellor training fall off my back as detached from the *experience* of training which is now integrated, and part of myself, and therefore not very giveable in terms of fact and descriptions.

And this tension between concrete facts and myself feels like another dichotomy that formed part of my training. This was the dichotomy between the training in skills, which was important and took up a great deal of training time, and finding out about myself, which could not be formalized as training although the training offered every opportunity for self discovery. Skills, after all, are important facilitators, and help to create the means of giving oneself in the relationship between counsellor and client. However, I now know that they can never substitute for the self in the relationship. So I had to find out about that self, and my being, in ways that were not related to skills training, important though that is.

This fundamental paradox of counsellor training, and indeed the counselling relationship, may be enacted here. For I am aware that I want to write a good chapter on counsellor training. But in the end, there is only me in this chapter; and I am at my worst when I want to do things with clients or act as their rescuer (Rowan, 1983, p. 37). When I start working with clients now I have learned to say that I cannot guarantee the outcome of counselling. Likewise I cannot guarantee the outcome of this chapter.

Course values

Thinking about being honest, or what I have learned to call 'congruent' or 'genuine' (Rowan, 1983, pp. 51–2) brings me back to the values, or philosophy, of the course I followed – values which are central to humanistic, person-centred counselling. In the introductory course material, as well as the poem, I found the following:

> The central *philosophy* of the course, an acceptance of Rogers' position on the 'self therapeutic capacity, and wisdom of clients', takes us primarily into humanistic, psychology and client-centred practice.

Like *Ithaka*, this means more now than it did then. I must admit that when this philosophy was offered to me in the course instructions, it had a tenuous intellectual meaning and no grip at all on my feelings. What happened to me as a trainee feels something like what may be the experience of being a client, in the early stages. When I start working with a client, what I offer as counsellor may often seem very slight and tentative. If I am lucky (or skilled) and the relationship develops, my hope is that the client, through the experience of being a client, will thereafter recognize respect for the core qualities of person-centred counselling. I also hope that these qualities will be accompanied by the client's *own* self-belief and self-respect. But the client does not know this when they start. Indeed, they may find these qualities unfamiliar, and difficult to recognize. As a counsellor, I try to stay with them, using my counselling skills and techniques, but also by being *myself* in the relationship. When I started counselling I used to wonder what earthly use this could be, and sought furiously for better technique, or expertise. I now know from experience that this element is crucial in the counselling relationship and will work more than my most accomplished skills. But I did not know this for myself at the start of training. So once again the course material and philosophy was out of time. It means more to me now that it did then, yet I had to have it then if I was ever to start learning. Referring again to the introductory material, I read the following:

> Personal development and self-awareness are considered to be central to the therapeutic movement in clients. The course takes very seriously the claim of Norcross and Guy [Norcross and Guy, 1989] based on a consistent research literature that 'the psychotherapist is the central determinant of clinical improvement'. By this they mean that the *person* of the counsellor, not her techniques or theories, is the key to liberat-ing the client's self therapeutic capacity.

This description was the course philosophy and therefore underpinning my training, even if I did not recognize it in the beginning nor fully understand its implications at the time.

As with clients, so with trainees, and vice versa. It may not be possible, in a life-enriching journey, to say accurately at what point chronologically certain things changed, or happened, or what techniques helped facilitate this. At best, however, trainees will be aware that change has occurred and lessons learned. They then go back to the start again, enhanced with new vision.

Myself at the start of counsellor training

In 1992, I was appointed as a chief executive in the National Health Service (NHS). At the start of counsellor training, three years later, this felt significant. I thought I was making a radical departure from management and towards practice, which is where most of my staff do their work. I felt very apprehensive. I suppose there is a kind of image (not always a very good image) that senior managers are strong, or even macho, people who are in control. Starting counsellor training was a big step forward in acknowledging that for me at least this is not the truth. It was a step (the first of many) towards acknowledging real vulnerability in others, and myself and of opening myself to it. I have moved many more steps towards vulnerability, towards being open, to being wounded. I do sometimes still think I must be crazy, for to be open to wounding causes pain. Much better to stay in the role. I found to my fascination others on the course also using, and then battling with the protection of their roles; nurses, CPNs, speech therapists, social workers. In my awe in the face of these practitioners I can see that I had attributed to all of them great skills in openness, sensitivity and so on. They after all are on the side of the angels, and managers mainly on the dark side. So when I was wrestling to lose my role (which I did, I think, pretty quickly) I learned a lot about myself – including the false stereotyping I had passed onto others in the caring professions, only to find they too were struggling sometimes to be real and to go beyond 'role'. What a relief! And what a significant piece of learning! How could I ever have thought it was only me that was not always 'real'? I apologize for the obviousness of this observation; I do feel psychologically 'dim' a lot of the time, but when insight comes it comes with great force!

I also thought being a chief executive was something I would need to tell people about quickly, unless I was to 'cheat' on them, since several trainees worked in other NHS Trusts, and I was also worried about confidentiality.

These anxieties seem really bizarre now. I soon discovered that being known as a chief executive had no bearing on issues of confidentiality. As soon as I behaved as the ordinary person I am, then this is what people reacted to, and have always reacted to, both positively and negatively. I know that I should not think anyone is bothered by my title. The fact that this has been quite a powerful experience says much about how I (and perhaps others) go around buried in armour, well protected, but missing the absolute experience, for good or bad, of being responded to as *myself*.

I had become divorced in 1993, and this seemed important too at the start of counsellor training. The end of my marriage was my first major effort to set boundaries, and to state what was, and was not, acceptable to me. I did it after I had been in counselling myself for some time, and I did it as an act of faith in the understanding I had gained, and also in the belief that I had to implement change in my life. From this point onwards it has been a journey, one in which I had no notion, at the start, of the pain that would be involved, nor of the gradually evolving understanding, and richness that sometimes came. And within a year, in 1994, that personal journey became, and remains, closely intertwined with the journey into counsellor training.

My motivation to train

One of my motives to train feels rather trivial in a book about counsellor training: I wanted to make new friends. After a term of night classes on upholstery skills, banging, clattering and stitching, but not talking, counsellor training seemed a way of making friends that would go beyond the superficial! And now I think about it, many of my fellow trainees, in our first week on the course, gave this as one of their motives to start training.

And I did find friends. Some have become very good friends. We have survived counselling together. These are friends who have openly and courageously offered themselves as clients for training purposes. They are people who have been tempered by the reality of living through, and dealing with the stresses, strains, and conflicts that training can bring. There is a special closeness and mutual sensitivity and understanding in these friendships. The experience has been, as a fellow trainee put it, 'like coming home'. To find friends such as these is such a relief, and such a pleasure. I can feel my shoulders relax while thinking about it.

Another motivation to train was my sense that I had benefited from counselling myself, and might be able to learn these skills for the benefit of others. I feel a bit uncomfortable about this, for it has the sound of the rescuer about it. Nevertheless, when writing our wants and needs at the start of the course, it was surprising how many of us had a similar motivation.

Now I work in another NHS Trust as a counsellor and I do help people, so I think I have to accept this motivation. When the outcome is good, it does feel surprisingly satisfying. But my helper motivation is tempered by a real recognition now that there are no *good* counsellors without *good* clients. I also know what I owe to my experienced, sane, compassionate and humorous supervisor. In fact the training never really stops; it is an ethical requirement to 'maintain on-going professional development' (BAC *Code of Ethics*, 1996, para. 2.4.2), and the wisdom of this requirement is absolute.

What I did not think motivated me in understanding counsellor training was a desire to do more academic work! I have a PhD (in eighteenth-century English literature), and when I started training that seemed enough. It was the practical skills that I was seeking; anything else was secondary and merely necessary to pass the course. I have therefore spent the last three years convinced that I am crackers at the start of each year, and comforting myself with the thought that I can always give it up. I do not know what defences that reveals in me, and what fears of not being found good enough remain! Because it seems to be as if everything I most shy away from is what I most need! For it is the academic and theoretical study, albeit combined most importantly with practical work, that I have enjoyed most. Now, to my surprise, the matter of working in an academic way is becoming important again as I approach my research year. I am learning that my attitude to academic work is an important area of personal development.

Personal development

Counsellor training took a chunk of my life and, at the end, I certainly felt older! In experiencing and thinking about my personal development, I heard and still hear ancient voices telling me that this emphasis on self is a bit self indulgent, really rather bad, a bit spoilt or showing off. But I have learned a certain kind of deafness. Counsellor training has taught me to understand that I was not only allowed to be myself, I positively had to be my real self if I was to be any use at all to clients. Although those ancient voices still call to me down the years I now know how to answer them: by holding on to the factual, rational justification for being oneself that counsellor training offers. But for me this realization was accompanied by the liberation of realizing that I was positively mandated to be myself, and that this self was highly valued. During my first year of training, I wrote in my learning record of seeing a red sports car cruising along the A19 with a number plate M1 5ELF, and the pleasure that had given me – and my tutor wrote 'Yes!' in the margin. This may not sound much of liberation to anyone else. I think, however, that many others and I have been taught (trained by ancient voices) to see ourselves as flawed, and the emanations from ourselves as bad, or worse. According to Carl Rogers (1951), this is the fundamental cause of so much personal distress. Counsellor training is about learning to give clients unconditional positive regard, as Rogers called it, so that they come to see themselves differently, not flawed, but prized. Ideally, the counsellor-training environment, too, should offer this support to the *trainee*; mine did, and the impact was enormous. Some days I could shout it from the rooftops, and now I know too, in an experiential way, what I am trying to create for my clients. It is not a magic wand, but it is life changing.

I owe much to the course. Ironically, it took place in the university where I came as an undergraduate in 1971, a skinny pre-anorexic 18-year-old. Being a student fed me in a number of ways. I found that I learned a way of undoing the tied-up sack I was in at that time, on the threshold of adulthood. I gained the liberation of knowledge, and indeed the literal wealth it can sometimes bring. However, what I never thought to do was to learn, from scratch, that I had value as myself, and that not valuing myself as a woman in her forties was a bigger tied-up sack than any I had ever known. Getting out of it still leaves me breathless, and unknowing (but learning) of the consequences of valuing myself. It is the best gift I was given by counsellor training; the best gift we can give our clients too.

The training experience

The gift was given through both the structure and the culture of the course. The structure was pretty consistent, term after term. Assignments and the term programmes of topics I knew little about all played into my desire for mastery and knowledge: I wanted to be a good well-informed trainee. Thus the central paradox of training was, and remains, how to be taught and trained, and yet also to let go – indeed how to learn to let go. My old self, tied up in a sack, went for being academically impressive, and my new, emerging self wanted to let go of that in order to experience my intrinsic worth. The tension of the paradox was a real challenge.

The course was organized so that each term had a pattern and a rhythm. Assignments across two years took the form of an essay on 'issues in counselling', a commentary upon a piece of skills work, sometimes presented to other trainees to encourage considered modifications in the light of their comments, and a case presentation also to a group of fellow trainees. There was a requirement to show increased levels of understanding and insight in all three areas, as the terms progressed, but the fundamental rhythm of the work was consistent. The course offered a great deal of freedom in the choice of essay title for the 'issues in counselling' section; thus the course philosophy of faith in, and respect for, the trainee, was sustained.

Tuition and lectures covered a lot of ground. There was an introduction to Carl Rogers and person-centred counselling, and a splendid term spent looking at the use of imagery and metaphor. Other topics included Gestalt therapy, psychodynamic theory, cognitive therapy, sub-personalities, personal construct theory, self and trauma, self and sexuality, note keeping, child sexual abuse, ethics, counselling and power, eating disorders, suicide, bereavement and loss, and so on. It was very thorough, and looking through my files I can see the grid of the timetable, an attempt to pass a net around my and others' experience, to capture it and pass it on. The contents of these boxes in the grid were both important and necessary, and indicated the road by which I was enabled to make my own personal journey. I arrived at a place where I could *unfocus* and experience my creativity. This I see as a necessary prelude to real empathy, one of the core conditions of person-centred counselling. John Rowan describes this as a condition in which we enter another person's world 'from his or her perceptual and emotional perspective . . . and put ourselves into the other person's shoes' (Rowan 1983, p. 49). He describes this process as starting with awareness, or openness:

> Rogers (1968) calls it 'intuitive sensing', and emphasises that it is the opposite of having clear-cut constructs – it is a whole person awareness, not just an intellectual awareness . . .

And

> It is hard to describe, but it seems that the essence of it is an openness to one's own experience as well as that of the others, in a context of action.

It entails a deliberate effort . . . to switch off one's usual state of consciousness, where one is trying to be sharp and accurate and focused. It is a kind of deliberate unfocusing . . .

I have described this at length because it is so central to my training experience. It was about focusing in order to be able to unfocus, gaining skills and then letting go. Everything in some way contributed to this process: it was training in the act of empathy. I once said to one of my tutors 'I never knew empathy would be so difficult'. Perhaps this was why so much of the course was focused on its development, focusing on ourselves and our personal and skills development, only to let this go in the actual act of empathy, of being open to experience (knowing oneself) in order to understand another.

Sensitivity group

Now I think I begin to understand the purpose of those strange sensitivity, or experiential groups that also formed a large part of my training! For they did feel strange to me initially, especially when I was earnestly hunting for skills and knowledge. Six or seven people sit in a room, and wait for someone to start talking. Wow! 'What is this about?' some of us wanted to know.

I think, for me, that it was about vulnerability, yet again, a vulnerability which perhaps has relevance for the client and counsellor. Where do I start? Do I start? What am I feeling? How can I respect others in the group? What if this bores me? I discovered that much of my vulnerability lay in something I do all the time, and that is talk! Sometimes it was hard, therefore, not to hold back as a way of preserving my defences, and keep myself intact. At the same time, an inner voice was saying there wouldn't be much benefit derived from talking my way to feeling safe – literally, no pain, no gain. Watching colleagues and friends in those sessions, it seemed as if the struggle might be the same for all of us, for there were some long silences – and the longer they were, the harder it was to break them! However, at times, one member would be almost bursting to tell something to others – and that seemed to occur naturally too, the collective recognition of an individual's need. And sometimes the need was joyous expression. I learned in a new way that sensitivity need not be synonymous with sadness.

But always I was reminded of the vulnerability involved in an encounter with another; every time I give myself, I am in the middle of the room, for acceptance or disposal, interest or confusion, liking or disliking – and so too for the other person.

I think, therefore, that I was most forcefully reminded of my own vulnerability, and thus that of the client – and why we need sensitivity to oneself and to the other. I hope again this does not sound too obvious. A mass of stories, feelings, emotions and sensitivities were spread out and shared in the group across our months together – so much so that we have kept in touch and still meet! But the important point remains that I needed the *felt experience* of exposing feelings, and vulnerabilities, receiving and understanding these in others, to know a little of where my clients are. I am profoundly grateful to the sensitivity groups for offering me this.

Doing weird things

Anyone contemplating counsellor training can expect to take part in some 'weird' activities. I am not sure what my management colleagues would think of group hugs! Well, actually, I think I am pretty sure, especially as I have an all male team, apart from me. They would think I was off my trolley! And I'm rather glad I am off my trolley these days, for I seem to be open to a wider range of experience than ever before. This is due, in part, to doing weird things.

For example, one term ended with a corn dance, another with a candlelit procession. On another occasion, the group made an image of the Snow Queen, after listening to that ancient and most meaningful story. I became passionately involved in making her beautiful, because I wanted others to feel the beauty that evil sometimes has. Nobody ever said the fallen angels were ugly – if they were we would all have given up on evil a long time ago. I needed to say this in the group, through my creation of the Snow Queen, to remind myself of energies and forces that sometimes cannot be wrestled down, and that may even be a necessary part of being human. I must have felt that night of the course that I wanted to remind others that counselling and therapy are not 'the bland making the unbland bland!' (Masson, 1989, p. 245). I do not know if I succeeded, but I certainly remember being very involved. This learning was reinforced when I read the following:

> *The Fairy Godmother*
> Woman of no substance. You stardust – sprinkled – everyone's
>   Guardian Angel.

Don't give me your easy empathy and closely-guarded positive regard.
Don't give me your neon – warmth nor your pitiful candyfloss
     counselling.
I can see *myself* only in reflections from a darker soul than yours.
You may be slightly bruised perhaps.
But seem to bear no deeper wounds within –
Whose faint echoes you might now draw upon to truly hear my suffering.
Anonymous (*BAC Counselling Journal*, 1994, quoted in Howard, 1996)

I did sometimes wrestle with feelings such as this, as a trainee, and indeed as a client, and the nagging belief that to be a counsellor is to be Fairy Godmother. But the darker side, personified by the Snow Queen, was part of the course. Across the deepening experience of my years of training, it has seemed to me that the last thing anyone wants from counselling is blandness, conformity, or lack of passion, though the energy required by tutors and trainees alike to banish theses dangers and take another route is immense. The course group was a very mixed bag, with latent possibilities for tensions that did indeed occur. I learned, with the help of the Snow Queen, that there is no better way of learning to respect others, to accept others and to be congruent. And in this learning, there was pain, as well as the rewards and a lot of fun.

Ending

A poem was an important part of my beginning to train as a counsellor. Another poem expresses what the training means to me now and what I learned. The poem is about giving and giving back. As a trainee, I gave back parts of myself to myself and learned that this is what I needed to do to become a therapeutic helper. Perhaps I did not know empathy would be so difficult because I did not know at the outset what was at stake.

And You, Helen
And you, Helen, what should I give you?
So many things I would give you
Had I an infinite great store
Offered me and I stood before
To choose. I would give you youth,
All kinds of loveliness and truth,
A clear eye as good as mine,
Lands, waters, flowers, wine,

As many children as your heart
Might wish for, a far better art
Than mind can be, all you have lost
Upon the travelling waters tossed,
Or given to me. If I could choose
Freely in that great treasure-house
Anything from any shelf,
I would give you back yourself,
And power to discriminate
What you want and want it not too late,
Many fair days free from care
And hear to enjoy both foul and fair
Any myself, too, if I could find
Where it lay hidden and it proved kind.

Edward Thomas, 1878–1917
(Thomas, 1964)

References

BAC, *Code of Ethics and Practice for Counsellors*, May 1996, para. 2.4.2.

BAC Counselling Journal, February 1994, quoted in A. Howard (1996) *Challenges to Counselling and Psychotherapy*, London: Macmillan.

Cavafy, C. P., 'Ithaka', in *The Complete Poems of Cavafy* (translated by R. Dalven 1961), London: Hogarth.

Masson, J. (1989) *Against Therapy*, London: HarperCollins.

Norcross, J. C. and Guy, J. D. (1989) 'Ten Therapists: The process of being and becoming', in W. Dryden and L. Spurling (eds) *On Becoming a Psychotherapist*, London: Tavistock/Routledge.

Rogers, C. (1951) *Client-Centered Therapy*, Boston: Houghton Mifflin.

Rowan, J. (1983) *The Reality Game*, London: Routledge.

Thomas, R. S. (ed.) (1964) *Selected Poems of Edward Thomas*, London: Faber & Faber.

5

Walking the Tightrope

Caroline Kitcatt

Caroline Kitcatt outlines the events which brought her into contact with the world of counselling and her motivation to seek formal training, following the breakup of a long-term relationship. She describes how she tackled the problem of financial restraint in order to take up a place offered to her at an institution a long way from her hometown. The salient features of the course are highlighted and particular focus is given to specific aspects, which proved to be significant turning points in the author's personal and professional development. The highs and lows of the training are identified as well as the sources from which the author was able to draw strength. A poignant note is struck with reference to the sense of abandonment experienced at the end of the course by the apparent indifference of the tutors and the difficulty of finding paid employment after qualifying.

My decision to train and work as a counsellor was made in 1991 when I joined NCH Action for Children's Careline as a volunteer telephone counsellor. This was the result of a lot of work I had done on myself following the breakup of a live-in relationship a few years earlier. In the devastation and despair that followed the break up, I had not had access to a counsellor, but had eventually found my way to a course called 'Personal and Professional Effectiveness for Women', which was instrumental in enabling me to look at myself and my life and make changes.

One of the changes that I wanted to make was to find out what I wanted to do with my working life. I had often been told I was a good listener and I wanted to feel that I could make a meaningful and positive contribution to life.

Careline was a general telephone counselling service open to all. I joined in April 1991 and the initial training had me sitting there terrified at my presumption in believing I could help. At the same time I had a deep conviction that this was what I was meant to do and that if I had the ability to make a difference I should use it.

I found myself with people who saw the world from a similar viewpoint, which in itself felt very powerful. I read as much as I could and took every opportunity to learn. I moved into working in education as an accommodation and welfare officer but soon realized that a caring role was not going to be enough. I wanted to work as a counsellor and so I needed formal training and qualifications.

It was shortly after starting to train for my Counselling Skills Certificate at evening class that I saw a newspaper advertisement for the one-year intensive full time diploma course at the University of East Anglia. At that time I was working full time to pay my mortgage and to support myself. I had planned to study at evening class and was not looking for a full time course. Despite the fact that I could not see any way I could possibly do the training, I sent for the prospectus and an application form.

When the prospectus arrived it seemed as if it had been written for me. Everyone I showed it to encourage me to apply, and so I decided to trust my intuition. I had tremendous support from my family and friends, and having been offered a place and accepted it, I put my house on the market and resigned from my job, borrowed enough money to survive on and moved from Kent to Norwich.

I can remember walking towards the education building on that first day feeling a sense of anticipation and excitement. As I walked into the room and introduced myself it felt very right to be there. There was a sense for me of 'at last!' After what seemed like a long time of wanting to work as a counsellor, this was going to be the final hurdle, or so I thought.

The first week of the course was an 'intensive week' when we came in every day for six days. In this way we got a feel for all the differ-ent learning experiences on the course and started to adjust to being in the group. There were 18 people on the course. Some time was spent in the community group, which was the whole group plus two tutors. We were divided into two groups for skills training and supervision, in addition to being allocated our own personal supervisors once we started seeing clients. We were also divided into two different personal development groups, which meant that we were each in small groups with all but four or five of the course members. A pre-course requirement was to write an autobiographical essay. This was shared in our skills/supervision groups with each of us taking turns to read these during the first week. This was a very powerful way of hearing from each other where we were and how we had come to be on the course. I found that afterwards I could not always remember details but I had a strong sense of each person in that group.

During that week we also had some theory and skills training complete with video, which I found very valuable, but I was aware that some course members found it hard to do. Throughout the course I felt confident in my skills base and that this was the time to learn and make mistakes. This meant that the skills/supervision group was where I was able to consistently contribute and be myself, despite growing problems with the community group and personal development group. I also enjoyed the theory lectures, and the written work, immersing myself totally in reading and learning. There were some lectures which I found less stimulating, generally where we had visiting lecturers talking about other approaches. This only served to re-inforce my sense that the person centred approach was right for me, and while I find other approaches interesting, they are not for me.

By the end of the first week I felt happy but very tired. I also found myself eating ravenously! The only thing that I found strange was that I hadn't found anyone in the group with whom I had 'clicked', which was unusual because I had always found on previous courses that I became close friends with at least one person. This never happened during the year of this course, but has since with particular course members, so maybe it was in the nature of the situation that close friendships simply did not happen for me in the normal way. Certainly we immediately got to know each other on a level which normally takes quite a time to reach, and this mirrors what often happens in the counselling relationship for clients, the difference being that with clients it is not reciprocal.

One group that I did enjoy was the pub group! Some members of the group would meet in the graduate bar after evening lectures and here we could laugh at ourselves and generally relax. There was a core of regular members, but at some time or another most of the group came along. It was a chance to get to know each other better away from the course, and, being in a new city and living alone, became the focus of my social life.

During the first term, I found that I had increasing difficulty in feeling safe in the community group. The group was made up of all ages and personalities and my initial confidence changed to confusion and vulnerability as I tried to work out what was going on in the group, both expressed and more particularly not expressed. The speed and intensity of experiencing in that group left me feeling I could not keep up. I had my perceptions challenged and felt unable to be sure what was going on. I allowed myself to be silenced and I also felt very scared at times. I was questioning everything and felt far away from all that was familiar. I now wonder whether, if I had not been so far away from friends and family, or if I had found some one in the group who shared my perceptions, I would have been better able to hold on to my sense of self and my own validity. As it was, towards the end of the first term I decided to ask for my own personal counselling to try to deal with all these feelings. Unfortunately, I had to wait and by the time I got to see a counsellor it was nearly the end of term. I had two sessions before Christmas and two after, by which time I felt more able to engage in the group setting and more able to stay with my feelings of confusion around what was going on in the community group. Although I found all this quite scary, I know it was excellent preparation for working with clients.

Client work began in the second half of the first term. One of the things that appealed to me about the course was that it provided supervised practice as an integral part of the course and we did not have to find our own clients. I also wanted to work as a student counsellor so the opportunity to work in the university counselling service was ideal.

I remember longing to be working with clients and not feeling too nervous about it. I felt challenged and excited by the prospect and very safe within the counselling service itself. The apparent simplicity of the person-centred approach belies its power and felt a bit like I imagine walking a tightrope with no safety net might feel. There are no techniques to bring in when things get sticky, and one of my tasks was to trust that I am enough if I can be myself offering a particular relationship and being with the client where they are.

My first clients were challenging in various ways. I found them fascinating and really looked forward to my personal supervision where I could explore what was going on and felt very validated. Some clients had experiences very close to my own and expressed feelings with which I could readily identify. I learnt to separate 'my stuff' from theirs, partly in supervision but also in the community group. The module on spirituality also started during the first term. I had been particularly interested in this aspect of the course because it seemed to me to be very relevant to the work I would be doing and also because of my own lifelong fascination with it. My own spirituality is expressed partly through the liturgy of the Anglican Church, although I would describe myself as on the edge and a doubter and a stumbler. This part of the course was a chance to look at other ways of expressing and exploring spirituality. I missed my garden, which had been a deeply spiritual place for me, and I found myself painting large paintings in acrylics, a medium I had never previously used. I expressed my experience of the course and my spirituality in this way. I don't think I moved on in my own journey very much, but it helped me to bring my experience of spirituality into my understanding of my work with clients.

The start of the second term found me feeling stronger and more confident in myself. I had been able to spend time with family and friends at Christmas, and also had time to process some of what had been going on for me.

I felt more able to engage in the personal development group, although as a group it continued to have problems all year. I felt this was due to a certain amount of manipulative behaviour, which went unchallenged in both this and the community group. We were all trying so hard to be accepting and empathic but had not yet understood congruence. As a result I feel that we became embroiled in layers of incongruence and got totally stuck. This again was a lesson in what can happen in the therapeutic process. However, I had begun to accept and integrate parts of me that I had learnt to suppress or express in other ways. For example, I expressed my frustration with members of the group away from the group, which felt safe, but was unproductive, but as the course moved on I was more able to discern what was 'my stuff' and what was not and to start to express that in the group in more appropriate ways. I became far more in touch with the flow of my own experiencing as the second term went on.

I continued to enjoy the theory and skills, and really became involved in my clients' processes. During this term, one of the written assignments was a case study of work with a longer-term client and for me this was by far the most powerful assignment I did. It involved keeping very detailed notes and tape recording sessions. This had the effect on me of feeling deeply connected to this client, and one particular evening I had the experience, having seen and written about my client that day, of feeling as if I had momentarily stepped out of myself and into her experiencing. I can only describe this as deep empathy or intuition, and it was so powerful that I asked for time in the skills group the next day to talk about it and was overwhelmed with the pain of what I had experienced in my client. I did not know what to do with this experience and it felt out of control and quite frightening. It occurred twice on the course, but regrettably not since. With the support of my tutor and the group I was able to explore what this experience meant and how I might use it in my work with this client.

There was constant stimulation from different themes, ideas, and theories, but I found that we were often only able to touch on subjects that I longed to look at in more depth. This was particularly so in relation to gender and sexuality, disability and also race and culture.

During the term, I began to work with more depth of understanding and I benefited from my personal and the group supervision and learned to use it well. At the end of term I commented in my learning journal that I felt I had learnt a lot in my practice, such as how not to be distracted by other people in the client's story, how to stay with their experiencing, when to pick up on things that clients have said and gone past, and how to be myself in the relationship. I wrote that I hoped I could build on this during the final term and consolidate it.

I was questioning and trying to understand my relationships, very involved in what was going on for my clients and me and generally totally immersed in the course. I was also starting to explore what being person-centred might mean for me.

Emotions ran high that term and there were several upsets and conflicts between members of the group. There was a lot of anger around, both expressed and unexpressed, and secrets, which were tremendously powerful. By the end I was tired, lacking in energy, and felt shell-shocked.

During the Easter break I felt very much in touch with everything that was going on for me, in fact it became quite deafening at times. I had learnt to stay in touch with myself while at the same time being in touch with what might be going on for others. In this way I found myself constantly monitoring what was happening and starting to discern what was really going on. I feel this is one very positive effect of sitting in community groups and that this level of awareness would have taken much longer to reach if I had only had my own therapy. I was also able to take the risk of expressing my perceptions in all the groups. As a consequence of this I became aware of my personal power and was fearful of using it. I was also aware of the reactions I produced in others, but at that point did not really understand why. Part of the work since the course has been to feel comfortable with my own power and able to use it effectively both inside and outside of the counselling room. Another part has been understanding why I sometimes produce very different reactions in others. I know I have moved on with this, but I do not think I am quite there yet.

My tutor described me as more solid and serene at the beginning of the final term. I think that was true and I was certainly much more confident in all the groups. I was also keen to tackle problem areas in role plays and make the most of the time I had left to challenge and stretch myself. There were more interesting lectures still offering tempting views of areas such as eating disorders and sexual abuse for future exploration. My relationships with one or two course members had begun to deepen and I think it was during the final term that the foundations of a few close friendships were laid. There was an emotional intensity about that term which was partly tied up in unresolved issues among course members. I remember feeling angry that our tutors had not sorted this out, but realize now that only we could do it because only we knew what had been going on, it was our responsibility. Unfortunately I feel we never really managed it and I feel a lot of ambivalence now about the group as whole.

During the course my relationships with my tutors changed from initial awe to respect and a more realistic appreciation. I found it particularly hard to really 'see' my male tutor, there was much in my past around male authority figures, but having voiced this and been accepted, I now feel we meet each other as we really are and count both my tutors as friends as well as colleagues.

In the final term we had to write our self-appraisals. In these we asked for feedback from tutors, supervisors, course members and if appropriate, clients. The process of receiving this feedback and writing the self-appraisal was very positive and I gained more insight from it about how I come across to others. Once we had gathered the feedback and written about all of the areas covered by the course, we had to state whether or not we felt we were ready to receive our diplomas. The final week of the course was another intensive week and one of the main tasks was to read as many self-appraisal statements as possible and to give feedback. It was a powerful and moving experience; not everyone felt they were ready and some chose to defer, but most of us felt we met the criteria.

During that term I felt empowered and full of anticipation about the future. It was the fulfilment of a dream and I longed to be working as a professional counsellor.

The end felt like an anticlimax. We had to wait another year for our graduation ceremony due to the late finish of the course and did not even have our names posted up. Some people were moving away and all of us were very anxious about finding work. I felt abandoned and rejected by my tutors and very angry that I now had no work. I had always had a regular income and this was the point when I really realized what I had done. One of the most frustrating things for me has been the difficulty of finding paid work. It is not that the demand or need is not there, but that jobs are being cut back, particularly in education, and competition is high. Additionally, many vacancies require applicants to be accredited or eligible for accreditation, which has meant needing experience in order to get experience and is yet another hurdle to overcome.

Eighteen months on I have some work as a student counsellor and some in an employee assistance programme as well as some voluntary counselling, but nothing is permanent and I am still searching for a full-time counselling post. It is still touch and go whether I can survive financially as a counsellor. I think at present this is the most profound practical effect the decision to train has had and it is not one I expected.

At times it is hard not to fall from frustration into despair and I have been fortunate that I have had enormous support and encouragement from my parents and from one particular special male friend who has always encouraged me to follow my dream. I have also valued friendships with certain course members. They share my ideals and values and understand where I am coming from. We can communicate on a very deep level. These friendships have developed more strongly since the course ended and have been a significant source of support.

In personal terms the work has continued, although at a slower pace. I am often struck by new insights and these have reached into every corner of my life. Counselling training has a tendency to upset close relationships, I think partly because of increased expectations.

My relationships are still essentially the same, the difference for me being that I am more aware of what is going on and able to voice my understanding appropriately. I have always had the sense that I see the world slightly differently from other people, and to find that I can use my perceptions and my intuition in my work as a counsellor in a healing way is very powerful.

I think the most profound emotional effect of training has been in my relationship with myself. I have a high level of self-awareness, I can hold on to my sense of self when I feel vulnerable and challenged, I feel more comfortable with my own power, but I also understand that I can be perceived as threatening in both my strength and my vulnerability.

I have been able to work with clients from a broad range of backgrounds and in different settings, which has been a valuable experience. I have found time and time again that faced with difficult situations both in and outside the counselling room, I have been able to refer back to my training and feel grounded. I feel I can offer a therapeutic relationship and allow myself to be challenged and stretched without losing confidence in my ability. There have been times when I have felt deskilled and times when the relationship has not worked, but I have been able to learn from this and move on.

The year I spent in training was definitely the best year of my life so far and I have never regretted it. Even in the darkest and most frightening moments I never doubted that this was what I wanted to do. I do think, however, that it requires determination and dedication to achieve and also considerable outside support.

6

A New World

Carol Kidd

What one gains from a course of training is very much an individual matter, but what Carol Kidd sets out to do in this chapter is to give readers who may be considering undertaking counsellor training some notion of how different components of the course can impact upon the student, their personal relationships and even wider aspects of their life. Jocularly, it is suggested that counselling courses might carry a health warning! The author frankly discusses the risks involved and demonstrates how her life and values changed in the course of her training, culminating in the break-up of her marriage. The outcome of all this is a new-found belief in herself and although the emotions of panic, excitement and dread are still around for her, these are now managed more successfully. The part played by supervision and personal therapy is duly recognized in this transformation.

My first introduction to counselling occurred some twelve years ago in a dusty, dingy room. A bespectacled and rather severe middle-aged woman encouraged me to tell her what I felt about such intimate matters as my rapidly disintegrating marriage, my parents (one dead and one distant), and my view of myself (poor, to say the least). I shudder now to think of some of the unprofessional ways in which this woman conducted our sessions and to this day I do not know what her training was. But in spite of some questionable practice, I feel I owe her a big debt. Not only did she help me to cope with desperate and suicidal feelings, but also that initial experience of the value of counselling was instrumental in opening up for me a whole new world.

A few years later, and once more a client (though different place, different counsellor), I took the decision to try sitting in the other chair, so to speak. I had been told often enough what a good listener

I was. Armed with that knowledge, and keen to learn more about the whole 'mystery' of counselling, I embarked on a six-week introductory course. Little was I to know that this tentative foray would escalate to five consecutive years of study and a dramatic change in career. Thus began a succession of counselling courses, culminating in an MA. However, the course that has had the most profound effect in terms of learning and changing was undoubtedly a two year part-time advanced diploma course, which is what I am going to concentrate on here.

My aim in doing this is above all to give readers a flavour of the *experience* of the diploma. While this is inevitably a personal and individual matter, I hope that there is sufficient common ground for this to be relevant to others undergoing, or planning similar training. In doing this I will be looking at the different components of the course and its influence on me, my relationships, my counselling, and ultimately, all aspects of my life.

My feelings as I embark upon writing this chapter are remarkably similar to those I experienced at the start of the course: a mixture of sheer panic (will I be good enough, will I cope?), excitement (where may this lead?) and dread (it feels too big, too overwhelming). The fact that I am still experiencing these feelings some five years later could be seen as a retrograde step in my personal development. However, the big difference now is that as a result of my training I have learned to master such feelings, insofar as they no longer prevent me from ploughing ahead regardless (as they often did in the past). Learning to take risks has been just one of the offshoots of the advanced diploma for me and as such is but one example of personal development occurring through training, as I hope to demonstrate in this chapter.

To embark on the course itself felt like a huge risk, both in terms of possible failure or inability to cope and in exposing myself to new and frightening experiences. The first day of the course is etched firmly in my memory as one of blind terror. There were shades of schooldays, in my conviction that everyone else would be more intelligent, more competent, more articulate than I was. I felt tongue-tied and inadequate in the warm up exercise and asked myself. Why do the others all seem so at ease, so able to talk readily to others in this assembled group of strangers?

I am glad to say that hurdles such as these gradually diminished in size during the two years, though if you were to put me back in the same situation, I still would not find it easy. The difference now is that I would be much more aware of how I was feeling and would be better able to dispute my irrational beliefs. A greater confidence in myself and a wish to continue self-challenging would help me to push myself forward more. So the panic would be there (in milder form), but the way I handle it would be different – not as different as I would like it to be in an ideal world, but I need to be realistic here!

Whenever I start to reflect upon my training as a counsellor, I find myself beginning to think in superlatives or clichés – a tendency that I will seek to curb, since it would not bode well for the readers of this chapter. However, there is no getting away from the fact that the two years of the advanced diploma has been one of the most dramatic periods of my life. I sometimes think the course directors should issue a health warning to prospective trainees! A facetious observation this may be, but on a more serious note, several of my fellow trainees have (like me) undergone dramatic lifestyle changes as a result of the course.

Personal development

Thinking back to the course, it is personal development that emerges predominantly in my mind and the initial emphasis of my reflections will be on this area. That personal development should lie at the heart of counsellor training seems appropriate to my work as a person-centred counsellor, in which the whole person of the counsellor is so central (Rogers, 1951; 1961).

In terms of personal change and growth, it seems fair to say that the two years of the advanced diploma outclass any other period of my life. Encapsulated within that change for me are several different areas, which I will expand on later. Briefly, they include the discovery of my innate ability as a counsellor, leading to the gradual emergence of a new professional identity, and a complete change of career, from journalist to counsellor. Alongside the development of my professional competence, and very much intertwined with it, has been the gradual blossoming of self-confidence and belief in myself. In this area I started virtually at rock bottom, so although I have climbed a long way, there is still plenty of scope for improvement.

I realize that the question of individual change as a result of training is a very personal matter, in that for somebody else embarking at a different starting point, some of what I experienced will be areas that have already been (or do not need to be) addressed. But I would expect that anybody who goes through a substantial course of counsellor training, such as the diploma, and enters fully into it will emerge significantly different at the end. The most important personal lessons I have learned from my training are: first, a new-found belief in myself, because I have succeeded and discovered a meaningful direction for my life; and second, the knowledge, on both intellectual and emotional levels, that I can take risks in allowing others to get closer to me.

An intrinsic part of my personal development throughout the course was a gradual increase in self-awareness. I recognize that there is no end to this particular journey and, of course, in this (as in other areas) it is hard to know how much to attribute to the training and how much would have occurred regardless. My own view is that those elements of the course designed to foster self-awareness certainly achieved their aim in my case. In saying that, I am thinking of the learning involved in receiving feedback from others, in learning how to monitor and assess myself, in the use of reflection through journal writing and in relating to trainees and staff.

My increased awareness left me with decisions to make regarding what I did with that deeper self-knowledge. Through my new-found commitment to counselling and to what could be considered a Rogerian desire to achieve my full potential, I have been determined to act on my awareness, a decision that has led to a mix of painful and pleasurable experiences in my constant challenges to myself. In marked contrast to my schooldays, when I did the minimum work required, I committed myself totally to the course and all its aspects, with what I must acknowledge to have been mixed motives. In part it was sheer pleasure in the learning and the academic work and in part a desire to excel and to prove to myself and to others that I could succeed. Because of my eagerness to develop both as a counsellor and on a personal level, overzealous commitment came easily to me. But, at times, being totally engrossed in the course undoubtedly had a detrimental effect on my personal relationships.

An inevitable concomitant of change is loss, and there has certainly been a heavy price to pay along the way, both in the realization of those parts of myself I would prefer to disown, and in more tangible terms, most notably the end of another marriage. I do not attribute the latter to the course itself (although my ex-husband may see it differently), because it accelerated rather than caused our alienation and separation. In weaker moments I would like to be able to revert to that stage of 'not-knowing' where I could pretend that all was well, and where I could take the easy option, rather than cope with the constant challenges and risks to which I have subjected myself.

Course components

Top of the list for me as far as risk and challenge were concerned was the group work. Normally I feel comfortable one-to-one, or in small groups, but sessions within the whole group of 16, or even in half of the group, started off as excruciating and finished off by being fairly excruciating. Not perhaps a great improvement, but this was an area I battled with throughout the two years (as reflected by the boring monotony with which the subject arose in my weekly journal). I constantly pushed myself to take risks – which to me felt huge, but to others might appear insignificant – and frequently failed to succeed, which invariably led to me giving myself a hard time.

During my subsequent two-year course (an MA in counselling in the same institution), I still felt tongue-tied and self-conscious if called upon to speak out in front of the whole group, and I am beginning to accept that there are limits to how far I can succeed in this area. This is offset by what seems a more valuable and positive personal outcome of the Diploma. I have learned to overcome my fear of rejection sufficiently to take risks with others on a one-to-one basis, both in initiating contact or relationships and in exposing more of my vulnerability. As a result, I am drawn closer to others. It is a measure of the distance I have yet to travel that I am still surprised when others do not reject me!

Hard though the group work was, it was as much an essential part of my training as a counsellor as were the skills training and the development of theoretical knowledge. Although there were times when the group seemed lacking in direction or clarity of purpose, participating in the group afforded me insights into how I was viewed by others, as well as greater awareness of what others felt. Perhaps we were fortunate that we all tended to be fairly measured and polite to each other, though conversely we could have learned more if we had been less sparing of each other's feelings.

The group work certainly engendered feelings of animosity and lack of co-operation in some members, principally those who had had 'unsalutory' experiences of groups in the past. The pressure to conform and to participate by revealing personal insights felt very powerful at times, and the knowledge that the group leader and members would be offering feedback on our participation removed a sense of autonomous choice. Even though I inwardly railed against this at times, it also prevented me from opting out and taking on the role of listener in group sessions, which is my natural tendency.

My journalistic training and experience afforded me a considerable advantage when it came to written work. It meant that, once I overcame the initial paralysis of fearing I would never write a 'good enough' essay, I both revelled in and excelled at the academic aspects of the course. The discipline of having to produce an essay, and my personal drive to perfectionism, meant that I learned a tremendous amount from the enforced reading and thinking around specific subjects. It is this form of reflective learning which particularly suits me, and which served to consolidate the practical aspects of the course.

Having said that, I was left with regrets at the end of the course about all we had *not* learned: the subjects missed out or skimmed over through lack of time. I remain in favour of a broad-based course such as the diploma at this level of training, rather than early specialization in one particular discipline, so that trainees emerge with a general grounding and are given a taste of different areas. However, there remains a risk of gaining a little knowledge in a lot of areas, and indeed it was my thirst for greater knowledge which led me straight on to the MA.

Interaction with fellow trainees within the structure of the course undoubtedly provided me with the greatest challenge and opportunities for learning. The training groups, where four of us would take it in turns to bring issues as clients or to counsel, helped me in two ways. The group provided a safe place in which to try out different ways of working, secure in the knowledge that feedback would be constructive, and with the reassurance that the 'client' would be taking responsibility for him or herself. That does not mean there were not times when a client would to his or her own surprise become upset. There was also the tension for the trainee when counsellor between wanting to help the client feel alright and following one's own training agenda for the session.

For me, a second learning aspect of these groups was in a way more incidental, in that having to bring personal issues to talk about in front of not one but three other trainees worked alongside the experiential group in encouraging me to open up more. Although

I was used to doing this in the context of one-to-one counselling, it felt more exposing when being observed, even though the principle focus was inevitably on the counsellor rather than the client.

'Performing' in the training groups, whether as counsellor or client, was especially hard to do in front of tutors, although the constructive feedback always proved invaluable, whether or not it was positive. In fact, there was often more learning in the negative feedback, although this was euphemistically presented as 'learning opportunities' rather than 'mistakes'. The tutors' unwavering support and belief in my abilities and potential certainly acted as a catalyst in the process of personal growth, as did the acceptance I felt from other trainees.

My interaction with staff on the course offered a valuable learning experience as well. While I never entirely overcame my deferential feelings towards the staff, and my desire to perform well in order to win their approval, I learnt a lot from them, perhaps above all through their example. This was the case not only when watching them in action, but also from their professionalism blended with humanity, their approachability, and their way of being with the trainees – no mean feat when you consider what a mixed bag we were!

As time went by, I was mostly able to take the staff down off the pedestals on which I had placed them, and to appreciate their individual strengths and accept their weaknesses. The fact that they declared themselves open to learning from us too played an important part in their becoming more human in my eyes. From the tutors, and from my own supervisor, I experienced a mix of support, acceptance and encouragement that felt incredibly liberating and a welcome change from earlier experiences of critical and demanding teachers at school.

The impact on client work

What about my clients? It seems that from the start I have come across to them as non-judgemental and non-threatening. I am aware that this can sometimes lead to a tentativeness in challenging which is perhaps too restrained, and a reluctance to be directive which is at times too extreme. I am often described as being calm or 'still', a semblance of inner peace which can at times mask a seething mass of emotions. I well remember the first client I had after starting the diploma, and it horrifies me to recall that she was a woman who had been repeatedly battered by her husband, and who was feeling desperate. I felt I was being thrown in at the deep end. For me, this raises an important issue both about assessment and allocation of clients to trainee counsellors (which was somewhat haphazard in the voluntary agency I then worked for), but also about the difficulty of untrained counsellors gaining the experience they need. More safeguards for the client, such as careful assessment and intensive supervision, costly on time though they are, could militate against the client acting as guinea pig. It certainly felt fraught with potential risk, although I sought to reassure myself that, with my modicum of training, and with the back up of the college and my supervisor, I would be offering the client more than her only other alternative – no help at all.

My increasing confidence and theoretical knowledge over the two years were reflected in my way of working with clients, and probably, the stages I went through are similar for all counsellors. They certainly concur with those identified by Stoltenberg and Delworth (1987), and have been neatly summarized by Inskipp (1996) as the shift from conscious incompetence to unconscious competence. So, first of all came textbook counselling with acute self-consciousness, which must at times be to the detriment of the client both in inflexibility and lack of focus on the client. I tried out lots of different ways of working in seeking to formulate my own integrated style. On some occasions, I tried something out specifically in order to be able to write about it for course assignments, a practice about which I had grave misgivings. Those were the times when it seemed more like a case of finding the client to fit the technique or approach, rather than vice versa.

It is only during the years since the course ended that I have begun to counsel more naturally, with more of an innate ability to do what feels right at the time. That is a far cry from saying that I always get it right, or that I do not reflect afterwards on different options, but it has become less of a consciously deliberate process. The point I have reached now as far as my counselling is concerned seems like a fair balance with a belief in my abilities, but tempered by frequent self-doubts. I console myself with the fact that if the time ever came when I lost those doubts, it would be a worrying day for my clients, since I might then feel I had all the answers. I prefer to believe, as Rogers (1961) suggested, that there is no end to what one continues to learn as a counsellor.

While the diploma served to launch me into further learning, it is also the case that freedom from the inevitable restraints of the course has led to a greater freedom to be more myself within my counselling work. However, I do not feel I could have continued my growth as a counsellor without the supportive environment afforded by training and the initial good grounding provided by the course. Part of that grounding has been an essential core knowledge of the underlying principles of counselling, which continues to underpin my work in spite of, or rather as part of, my individual approach. One measure of how I have moved on since the diploma is my decreasing pre-occupation with identifying the stages Egan uses to define counselling. These stages provided an invaluable map to help me find my way through the process at first, but using them became increasingly superfluous as they have merged gradually with who I am, my own unique style, and all that I bring to my work as an individual.

To use myself within the counselling relationship, as I can now do, is an essential part of my work as a person-centred counsellor (Mearns and Thorne, 1988). I do not believe I could have even begun to do this without the personal growth and self-awareness that developed during the diploma. This greater use of myself when counselling has been a part of my evolving way of working, which again has been a gradual change. At one stage immediacy and/or self-disclosure felt much too frightening, whereas now they come more naturally and I can see how this works towards encouraging greater openness creating greater equality within the counselling relationship.

However, I have to a great extent focused on personal development, and I feel I need to redress the balance somewhat by emphasizing the importance of the skills training, and the theoretical input from tutors, from fellow trainees, and in large part through personal study. All this has been closely bound up with learning a new way of being and has furnished me with the techniques and the knowledge which inform both the way I am in the therapeutic relationship and the additional methods I employ in order to offer greater flexibility to my clients.

The wider impact of training

My training has, perhaps inevitably, influenced my way of relating to others outside the counselling room. I find I most enjoy time with others who want to talk on a relatively deep and personal level, and am less attracted to superficial chat. That makes me sound more serious and intense than I think I am, since having fun is important to me too.

People often ask me how I can cope with listening to clients' depressing problems all day and I blithely assure them that I can only do it because I am almost always able to switch off from the client's problems at the end of the session. This is usually (but not always) the case, and I am sure stems from training in empathy and objectivity: the ability to get alongside without getting immersed in the client's issues. Of course there are exceptions, usually in cases of countertransference, and where I share issues or characteristics with the client. However, I find that the exceptions provide a useful criterion in deciding which clients to discuss in supervision. Having said that, there is no denying the fact that counselling is an emotionally exhausting job, though one which can bring with it great rewards, for the counsellor as well as the client.

I have found that being a counsellor increasingly permeates my whole being whether or not I am at work. My experience is that the more of myself I use within my counselling, the more difficult it is to differentiate between me the counsellor and me the person. This results from a finer tuning of my intuition, so that it is almost second nature to listen out for the hidden meaning or the non-verbal expression, whoever I am with.

I am not entirely comfortable with this facility, because although I would never attempt to counsel my friends or family, it introduces an inherent inequality into such relationships, and begs the question of what I do with that intuited 'knowledge'. There have certainly been times when friends and family have shared their troubles with me and I, as a counsellor, have seen ways to help that feel inappropriate to our relationship. At times, these two parts of me do not fit comfortably and perhaps make me more self-conscious than I would otherwise be about how I respond. I recognize too that there may be occasions when friends or family choose not to share their personal concerns or feelings with me for fear of being on the receiving end of involuntary counselling.

Another way in which my counsellor training has had a bearing on my life and my relationships is that through being more self-aware, I have become more able to be open about my feelings with others. This seems to be a case of inadvertently leading by example and more than one friend has commented appreciatively on the way in which this example has encouraged her to be more open herself. I have also found that in being less guarded I am at last learning the lesson that this draws others to me, and while I regret it did not happen earlier in my life, it makes me optimistic about the future. I am aware that this is sometimes on my agenda with clients, in encouraging them to develop closer support networks and open up to others, a proselytizing which may not always be appropriate, since it could be regarded as inadvertently seeking to impose my own values.

It seems significant that I first became involved in counselling through my own experience of being a client, and I sometimes think that if I had not had so many personal problems in my own life I would not be in a position to empathize and help others to the same extent – in fact I would probably never have contemplated doing so. In other words, I am a good example of what is described as a 'wounded healer' (Goodbread, 1997).

It seemed inevitable to me that the self-exploration and personal growth during the course would raise unresolved issues. This resulted in my choosing to put myself back in the role of client again, and I have continued in therapy for much of the five years since then. The difference this time has been the deeper level on which I have felt ready and able to work, exploring aspects of my formative years and so gaining an understanding of my behaviour patterns and ways of relating (to myself and to others). This leaves me with choices about whether to attempt to change those old, often self-defeating, patterns; and the in-depth nature of this work helps me to distinguish therapy from counselling, which I see as predominantly learning to cope in the present, with limited gains in self-knowledge.

Although receiving counselling was not mandatory on the diploma, I personally believe that counsellors should have at least some experience as a client, and that it is not possible to work with a client at a level deeper than the level one has worked at oneself.

The uninitiated might consider extended periods of therapy to be self-indulgent in the extreme, but I see my ongoing therapy as playing a vital part not only in my continuing personal growth (a necessary concomitant of developing further as a counsellor), but as a means of benefiting my clients indirectly, through my expanding awareness and my work on personal issues. A consensus among counsellors on the value of therapy for counsellors emerged from research I undertook during my MA, and is also reflected in the new BAC criterion of a minimum of 40 hours therapy for accredited counsellors.

Conclusion

My experience of the diploma was predominantly positive. That is not to say that there were not times when the demands felt too much, the piles of books too high, the constant juggling of different pieces of work too difficult. Yes, there were some weeks when I went home thinking 'I don't know why I bothered', or 'I got nothing from that today'. However, it was seldom if ever that on reflection that I failed to realize how much I *had* learned. This is indicative of my natural learning style, which is as a 'reflector' (Honey and Mumford, 1992). I need time to assimilate and ponder on what I have learned and experienced. This meant that for me the weekly learning journal was both a treat to be anticipated with relish and an invaluable source of learning.

Where am I now, some five years later? I am still deeply committed to counselling and convinced of its value, although by no means for all people or every problem. During those five years I have shifted from seeing counselling as all good, through a period of extreme negativity, to a point where I hold a more balanced view. Having recognized that I had become *too* immersed in the whole field of counselling, I have now achieved a better balance between counselling work, studying, talking about counselling, and the rest of my life.

For me, being part of the diploma group was a unique experience, and as a result I made several very close friends, as well as a wider circle of other good friends. I felt there was something about the intensity of the course, which seemed to strip away a certain amount of the formalities and pretensions behind which we all hide, and so enabled us to get on with the business of sharing ourselves more readily. I concede that there was certain artificiality about this, in that it was only a small part of our week that we shared. But a bond was forged, in some ways reminiscent of the counselling hour, which forms such a small but important part of the client's week. In the light of this, it was hardly surprising that the end of the course was difficult, and that there is a core nucleus of the group that still meets regularly.

I certainly felt bereft at the end of the course. Suddenly it was over, and I was forced to face the opportunities I had failed to take, the relationships I had failed to make. I was desperately anxious to extend my work within counselling, but afraid that no opportunities would present themselves. The latter still remains a fear and a pressure, compelling me to at least seriously consider, if not actually apply for, any counselling work that materializes. If training courses continue to churn out counsellors at the present rate, it is possible to envisage the situation escalating into too many counsellors chasing too few jobs (in fact, this is becoming increasingly the case in the area in which I live and work).

Having committed myself to three part-time counselling jobs when I finished the Diploma, I later had the courage to jettison one of them in favour of trying to build up a private practice. This is a prospect with little security, and with an increasing number of counsellors doing the same, I have found that the private work very much tends to fluctuate. I know others in the same area that have tried and not succeeded. I would certainly not give up all my paid employment in order to pursue private work.

Where to from here? If I were to do an Egan preferred scenario, I would paint myself a fantasy picture of secure employment as a counsellor, with support from like-minded people, but counterbalanced by close relationships and other interests outside the counselling field. The time is certainly right for a break from academic work after the MA, although I could see myself exploring more experiential training at a later date. I sometimes wonder if counsellor training can become addictive! I would like to extend the breadth of my work, possibly in working as a trainer at a basic level and by combining my journalistic background with my counselling in some way. It feels like the journey is far from over ... !

References

Goodbread, J. H. (1997) *Radical Intercourse: How dreams unite us in love, conflict and other inevitable relationship*, Portland, OR: Lao Tse Press.

Honey, P. and Mumford, A. (1992) *The Manual of Learning Styles, 3rd edn* Maidenhead: Peter Honey.

Inskipp, F. (1996) *Skills Training for Counsellors*, London: Cassell.

Mearns, D. and Thorne, B. (1988) *Person-Centred Counselling in Action*, London: Sage.

Rogers, C. R. (1951) *Client-Centred Therapy*, Boston: Houghton Mifflin.

Rogers, C. R. (1961) *On Becoming a Person*, Boston: Houghton Mifflin.

Stoltenberg, C. D. and Delworth, U. (1987) *Supervision, Counsellors and Therapists*, San Francisco: Jossey-Bass.

7

Singing Out

Suzanne Keys

This is largely a reflective chapter where Suzanne Keys draws out some inter-esting relationships between the practice of counselling and other activities in a person's life. For example, a parallel is drawn between counselling and for-eign language teaching; both are concerned with helping people to find their voice. Similarly, the relationship between the development of congruence and the growth of personal integrity is carefully worked out. Exploring the spiri-tual dimension is another important element in this chapter for, as the author points out, there is more to counselling than the counsellor–client relationship. 'Along with sexuality, spirituality is constantly present in our relating and it cannot be ignored. The place of love in the counselling relationship is exam-ined as well as the polarities of 'being' and 'doing'.

Counselling training for me was an experience of blossoming and find-ing a niche. I discovered a voice whose vibrancy surprised and delighted me but whose elusiveness dismayed me. At times I wailed and croaked and at other times I sang. It felt both new and familiar: a voice rediscovered under a lifetime of defences and survival tech-niques, reassuringly comfortable and solidly embedded in the core of my being. Through the process of challenging my assumptions about myself, my relationships and my world views, I became a pro-fessional. This journey was not dissimilar to a therapeutic process: passing through disintegration with its consequent feelings of being de-skilled, confused, lost and anxious towards a questioning of who I am and what I am doing, and then towards a new, more honest and anchored sense of myself and my capabilities. Often when I finish a counselling session now, six months on, I want to sing, skip and dance, because I know I am doing something I am skilled and trained in and about which I am constantly learning. In this chapter, I outline the background to my choice of career and training course. I then explore the most significant lessons learned from this important part of my life. To anticipate, these lessons relate to several themes:

- the wonder at belonging to a life-cycle and a deeper continuum
- the vulnerability of declaring a commitment to relationship and revealing intimacy, both sexual and spiritual, in public
- the pressures of wanting to please others and gain their approval
- the enjoyable naivety of believing in love against all odds
- the joy of acceptance of one another
- the unbearable process of self-doubt and questioning before speaking out with confidence and integrity.

These themes have emerged as I look back at my training experience through the lens of having recently got married. If I had not been through the transition of marriage, I would not evaluate my training as I do, and likewise my understanding of marriage would have been very different if I had not just finished counselling training. Both these life-changing events have formed who I am today as a person and a professional.

I conclude the chapter, from my current frame of reference, with the struggles of looking for work as a counsellor.

Why counselling?

I studied modern languages at university. With hindsight, I can see that in some respects this was a fitting preparation for working as a counsellor: both involve a curiosity to know how others communicate and an interest in different cultures and subcultures. Using a language that is not my own has often highlighted the significance of non-verbal communication. More importantly, being bilingual has helped me recognize the assumptions I invest in words and often make about people as I listen to them talk. Learning a second language has given me an appreciation of the uniqueness of an individual's personal language.

As an English teacher in the Ivory Coast and in France, I worked with groups and individuals, encouraging and helping people to speak out and find their voice in another language. Much of this was to do with enabling people to have confidence and trust in themselves. I also became involved in different helping relationships with people in hospital and particularly those living with the HIV virus and AIDS. I studied palliative care and this led to becoming involved in bereavement counselling. I also sought out counselling for myself when the balance between giving and receiving became too hard to hold. This first therapeutic relationship, in the role of client, was my introduction to the person-centred approach: experientially through feeling safe, accepted, respected and understood; and intellectually through the works of Carl Rogers (1951) and Mearns and Thorne (1988).

Which course?

Upon my return to England I started looking through the vast range of counselling courses on offer and talking to people involved in the profession. I was advised to 'do a BAC accredited course' and 'don't expect to get a job out of it'. Nevertheless, I was not discouraged and persisted in finding a course that felt right and fitted me best, even though it was not at that stage accredited (as it is now). I had to take out a loan to do it and leave my home in London.

There were three principal reasons why I chose the course. First, I wanted to root myself in the person-centred approach and not spread myself out in 'pick'n'mix' eclecticism. I believed this would give me the confidence and competence to practice, and to appreciate properly the differences among therapeutic approaches. And, indeed, it has enhanced rather than hindered dialogue with people who counsel in other ways. Second, although the profoundly challenging experience of counsellor training needs filtering and digesting, I wanted the intensity of a one year full-time immersion and the integrated experience of theory and practice, and individual and group learning. It was often the relentlessness of the pace that forced me to face uncomfortable issues I would rather have avoided. However, the most important reason for choosing this course was that it gave the opportunity to explore the spiritual dimensions of counselling.

Spiritual dimensions

From the beginning there was permission and encouragement to talk about beliefs, faith, religion and spirituality. The most powerful of our weekly community meetings was held in a room next to the holy shrine of a fourteenth-century Christian who wrote an incredibly insightful account of her relationship with God. She spent most of her life living alone in one room, where she was visited by people drawn from far and wide to speak to her.

Within the group there was a great diversity of religious background and spiritual belief. I discovered through my own experience of sharing snippets of my prayer life, for example, and hearing others speak about how they expressed their spiritual being, that these issues are some of the most intimate and often the most difficult to talk about. As a person and as a counsellor to leave these areas unacknowledged and unexplored is ultimately disrespectful to our clients and ourselves. Along with sexuality, spirituality is constantly present in our relating and it cannot be ignored. My training helped me to be more aware and less afraid of this dimension of my relating to my clients.

This manifested itself in practical ways too. I remember a skills group, for example, when we discussed how we each prepared for being with a client. Despite the different spiritual beliefs in the group everyone shared the concern of how to be most 'present' to the client. When I rushed from one client to the next I often did not connect with the person sitting in front of me. I discovered how important it was for me in my professional practice to take time to anchor myself through prayer, to be aware of myself, the client and our relationship. It was a way for me to focus on trusting the process and entrusting the relationship to God: a reminder that there is more to the relationship than the counsellor and client. In a very physical way I found going to the toilet, washing my hands in cold water and then having a good stretch help me to be present. I learnt from others that moving around the room, clapping in the corners after a client had left changed the energy in the room, cleared my mind and allowed me to be ready for the next client. During the year I became increasingly attentive to body language and responding to feelings in my body.

Belonging

Throughout the course I grew in my understanding of relationship. This was partly due to a growing sense of belonging, both to humanity and community. The acceptance of this belonging often felt risky and daunting.

Belonging to humanity means belonging to a continuum of which I had never previously felt a part. In our society, the continuum is marked by such rites of passage as birth, family, marriage, job and death. As I began to feel secure in a life cycle I had several powerful experiences in the course group and with individuals, clients and colleagues, of a deeper belonging. At the end of the course this was greatly facilitated by a visiting Japanese professor of person-centred counselling whose presentation of his native spirituality enabled me to feel more deeply connected to a current linking me to others and the world. I realized that love passes through me and that it is an illusion to think that I can turn it on and off and control it. It was a relief to realize that I was not responsible for generating love but for getting in tune with it: not mine to give or receive. Carl Rogers writes of a 'formative tendency', a universal driving force towards fulfilment and integration which is echoed in each individual's 'actualizing tendency' (Rogers, 1951): we do not have to push ourselves to grow, the potential and yearning is there within us to be unearthed and nurtured.

The central hypothesis of the person-centred approach:

> ... is that each person has within himself vast resources for self-understanding and for constructive changes in ways of being and behaving, and that these resources can best be released and realised in a relationship with certain definable qualities. (Rogers and Sandford, 1989, p. 1483)

In belonging to community I learned about these qualities of 'realness, caring, and a deeply sensitive non-judgmental understanding' (ibid.). It was not easy. At the beginning of the course I spent a lot of time feeling isolated because I did not feel 'heard': I imagined that no-one could understand or respond to me adequately, and perversely I pushed away any attempts to do so. Gradually, with help, I began to recognize that this was a self-destructive pattern that alienated me from what I most desperately wanted.

Much of our work on the course took place in a group in which there was nowhere to hide and where an awareness and acceptance of difference was paramount. I was challenged to accept myself: my uniqueness, my right to a voice, my inevitable weaknesses and strengths. It was hard to show myself unconditional positive regard and accept, for example, that I had prejudices. It did not fit with my view of myself as open-minded and non-judgemental. I am slowly learning, however, to chastise myself less. Instead of running away from difficult feelings and situations I am less afraid to ask myself what is going on, less accusatory and more gentle and loving. I was forced to learn this also through my work with clients. It was only three-quarters of the way through the course that I felt the difference for the first time between taking something personal and looking at it from a more curious and interested perspective. One of my first clients wanted to see another counsellor after two seemingly good sessions with me. Cognitively, I knew it was not necessarily my fault but emotionally it tapped into not feeling good enough, feeling rejected and a failure. By the end of the course, although my response to cancelled sessions included some questioning of my role in the relationship; I was more able to believe in the complexity of the issues involved. Not taking it personally does not mean distancing myself but rather being more present and more aware of the relationship. It also means being more freely able to move around in the client's world without getting caught up in my own feelings. As the year progressed I developed more of an idea of what empathy felt like rather than understanding it purely intellectually. It felt qualitatively different to actually be in the client's world rather than imagining or supposing or assuming what their world might be like.

Belonging to community also means that diversity can lead to conflict and awkward feelings about other people. In a group of twenty this is inevitable. My view of myself was that I was a caring and nice person and therefore to express negative feelings about somebody else was nasty and unacceptable. I developed my congruence in terms of being able to tune into what I was feeling and expressing it appropriately. I am still learning to trust that my intention is not to hurt others and that human beings are not by nature malicious. This also meant hearing how others perceived me without assuming the worst and without using their feedback to confirm a deep-seated fear that I am worthless.

Incredibly, through my training, I discovered in fact that a greater fear for me is that I do have worth, that it is acceptable to sing out and that I am loveable.

Love

The faith, trust and belief in one's own and another's resources in the counselling relationship are awe-inspiring. Learning about love was central to my training course: admitting and celebrating love in relationship, accepting that love inevitably brings with it hurt and loss, learning to receive without feeling obliged to give back. How easy it is to understand how a client can be overwhelmed by the warmth of a counsellor and how hard as a counsellor to acknowledge the thanks of a client without brushing it aside. Accepting the gift of love given unconditionally is one of the most difficult things to do and yet as a Christian this is central to my beliefs. God's love is generous and without conditions. If I find it so hard to accept, how can I hope to offer it? Can I give without the condition that it is received? I am still struggling with the complex nature of the conditionality of the counselling relationship.

If I believe in a God who has created me and loves me as I am then I am 'good enough' in his eyes. A huge learning for me in counselling training was in terms of accepting being a 'good enough' counsellor. I cannot be perfect, yet I want to improve. Despite my awareness of the weakness and fallibility of my humanity, I strive towards my potential for the divine.

Integrity

I was struck during training by how dearly I valued integrity. This spiritual quality is to do with being in touch with myself, listening to it and being true to it: not pretending and lying to myself when it might seem easier, not doing or saying things just to please others and be liked. Being genuine means trusting my own sense of right and wrong and valuing myself without using what I think others' yardsticks might be. It is a constant struggle to remember that my worth as a person is not dependent on others' approval and judgements. To be a good counsellor I do not need to please my clients and be liked by them and yet it is amazing how often this condition can slip in. This is where person-centred theory helps to identify the conditions of worth a person grows up with: such as 'I will only be loved and accepted if I please and help others'. In reality during training this meant that I had to struggle hard not to automatically respond to someone in need. It also led to a questioning of my motivation to be a counsellor. Do I simply want to rescue people from their problems in order to feel good about myself? Can I be happy 'being' rather than 'doing'? 'Doing' is signified by rushing in to help and to find answers and rescue someone from distress and 'being' is to do with trusting the unknown and the transcendent, staying with confusion and not measuring success through achievements and out-comes. Learning 'to be' rather than feeling compelled 'to do' is deeply counter-cultural as is striving to be genuine in all relation-ships. It is expected of all of us in certain circumstances to say we are coping and achieving however far this may be from how we are actu-ally feeling.

I am acutely aware of the importance of our social context in how we feel and behave and how much we may feel we need to conform to survive. One of the hardest things is to trust that the client knows what is best for them. Even if I value self-awareness and the explora-tion of feelings this may not be the way forward for the client. They know how much they can risk at any stage in their lives. I have to be aware of just how profound the repercussions of a counselling rela-tionship can be on people's lives.

Process

Like counsellor training, the therapeutic process is costly. It is emo-tionally draining and unpredictable. It is not straightforward, linear or even directional. I experience it zigzagging and lurching from insight to confusion and doubt and back again. There is a crumbling of all that is known and secure, a deep questioning of what has been taken for granted, a desperate feeling of isolation, entrapment and rootlessness, glimmers of hope and joy and yet a belief and a trust borne out that this was all somehow part of the journey to where I was headed. The challenge is staying with the process even if it seems contradictory, crazy and unbearably difficult and to carry on trusting that dis-integration does in fact lead to re-integration.

Conclusion

Looking for work now the course is over has taken me right back to the beginning of my training: feeling deskilled and questioning my ability. Yet I also have an energy and an enthusiasm and a deeper, stronger belief in myself. I know that I have those experiences behind me and even though every job application seems to ask for yet more experience plus accreditation and specialization I do feel I am starting from a secure basis.

Acknowledging the importance of community, I was keen to link up with other person-centred practitioners in my area as soon as

I could and this has become a lifeline of support and contact. It is reassuring to know that there are people beyond the training environment who are living and working in a person-centred way and earning a living from it. I am gradually building up my counselling hours through unpaid work and I have passed the milestone of my first paying client.

I am a beginner again with all the anxieties that go with being in this challenging position. Without the stimulus and nurturing of the training environment it is hard to find my voice and have the patience to trust that I will find a place where I fit.

References

Mearns, D. and Thorne, B. (1988) *Person-centred Counselling in Action*, London: Sage.

Rogers, C. R. (1951) *Client-Centred Therapy*, Boston: Houghton Mifflin.

Rogers, C. R. and Sanford, R. C. (1989) 'Client-centred psychotherapy', in H. I. Kaplan and B. J. Sadock (eds), *Comprehensive Textbook of Psychiatry*, Vol. 2, 5th edn, Baltimore: Williams & Wilkins.

8

Two Legs Good

Nikki Kenward

After several years as a successful actor and director, Nikki Kenward contracted a rare and serious illness which resulted in her becoming a permanent wheelchair-user. In this chapter she recalls her experiences of embarking on a counsellor-training course and the reaction of the institution, including tutors and peers, to her predicament. This is a very touching story, told with a mixture of humour and pathos, leading up to her decision to withdraw from the course prematurely. There are several important implications for disabled students and those who teach them.

'All animals are equal, but some are more equal than others'

(Orwell, 1945)

This is the chapter no one will want to read. This is the chapter that is different, because I am different, because I do not fit, and I cause problems, I make people uneasy.

I am something they hope they will never be. I am pain, I am need, I am sadness, pity and derision. I am without hope, incurable. I am the future you would run away from. I am the face to which you offer a meaningless smile. I am not equal to you; you are more equal than I.

Choose now. Do you read on? Or do you smile and turn away?

It is the first day of the course. I am wearing red, for danger maybe or for blood, I do not know. But I am here. It has taken me six years to take up the place I was originally offered to do the Dip/MA in counselling. They have moved the first meeting to a different room. I am late now; I cannot find it. We push open the door; there is a circle of people, they all turn. I know about circles. I have performed in them, held workshops in them, studied their ancient naturalistic roots. This is old stuff for me – powerful stuff! A circle is a space where anything can happen, as Peter Brookes said in his book, *The Empty Space* (Brookes, 1972), the space that we can fill with meaning. I make my entrance, the door bangs back, I am good at this, I know how to gain attention. 'I am not afraid', I tell myself. I have their attention. 'Making my entrance again with my usual flair', to quote Sondheim (1985).

A voice I know well says, 'There's room over here by me'. I wheel myself round, the last to arrive and sit by my friend, glad of her voice, her presence. 'We're just going round introducing ourselves', she says.

They carry on. They look clean for the most part, very clean. That is the word that comes to mind – very clean. Very clean, very white, very wholesome. No one like me, no one blind, or without a limb, no one of restricted growth, but they will all be disabled in some way, afraid like me, struggling with something or someone. There will be common ground.

All of us take our unfinished business with us to days like this. We are the students; they are the teachers. I study the body language; some looking down while still saying their piece, others look out of the window, and others clasp their hands or fidget with something. Not many address the whole circle, but some look to those gathered by me as they speak.

I ask those near me, 'What about you'?

'We're the lecturers', comes the reply.

I want to laugh. 'So what?' I think to myself. 'Tell us why you're here'. For a moment I am in school, we are in school, looking for the leader, the teacher.

In our fear, our excitement, we hang on to our bags, we may have labelled our belongings, our business is unfinished.

First day at school
A millionbillionwillion miles from home,
Waiting for the bell to go (to go where?)
Why are they so big, other children?
So noisy? So much at home they
must have been born in uniform.

I wish I could remember my name.
Mummy said it would come in useful
like wellies when there's puddles.
Yellow wellies. I wish she was here.

I think my name is sewn on somewhere
perhaps the teacher will read it for me.
Tea-cher. The one who makes the tea.
R. McGough (1976)

I'm far from home, I'd love a cup of tea, I'm thrilled to be here, but I've a feeling *they* don't make the tea. Who makes the tea here when you've stopped crying? Us? I wonder.

A few weeks after the term started I read this poem to the group. There was general agreement that it spoke well of our feelings on that first day.

When I was 12 and besotted with film and theatre, my escape from the drunkenness of my father and the pain of my mother's life became a full-fledged desire to act and not just a way of creating a reality more acceptable to my huge energy and active imagination. My mother pushed me through the door of the little grotty theatre in our town and said, 'Go on then ask. Ask if you can do anything'.

She never ridiculed my desire to act, although it must have come as some surprise from the child who hardly spoke till the age of seven but then, perhaps, she remembered my escape from the caravan we hired in Towyn, following a visit to the cinema to see Hayley Mills in *Whistle Down The Wind* (Bell, 1997).

'I've run away to be an actress', I wrote.

My father advised that I be left alone to go my own way. But my mother, worried by the traffic, discovered me, teddy bear under arm, heading full pelt for the bus stop outside the campsite.

So there she was, my mother. My father had died from drink three years previously. Making my dream a reality, she pushed me through the door of the theatre. I had found my place. I became a member of the Youth Workshop and got myself some Bohemian friends, most of whom were, in some way, misfits like me.

This was the 1960s, a time of encounter groups, self-development, trust games, relaxation exercises, all those things that Theatre Work-shop had developed and much later psychologists, counsellors and therapists were to put to use. I lapped it up. I had come home. I belonged. It took many more years before I realized the impact these times would have on my interest and work in counselling.

One of the characters in Samuel Beckett's play *Endgame* (1958) speaks these words: 'You cried for night. Now cry in darkness.'

I have cried in darkness many times in my journey, when I literally was blind and when I was blinded by emotion. There was much more to come before I could begin to learn to cry out for myself.

And so, I've always been a dramatist, always watched people. Now here, thirty years on, I am watching people on those two induction days of the Dip/MA course. There's me in my wheelchair, and all the others, about thirty of them, standing about. I can look back and rerun the scene. I am part of it, part of the joy, the fear, the excitement of new friends, new knowledge, and new pain. Now I see myself, I understand more, I understand I didn't listen to the moments, those moments of pure spontaneous thought when your brain works out the whole situation for you and provides you with a flash of thought, call it intuition, knowingness, what you like, but generally we ignore them. I didn't allow myself those moments. I whistled in the wind.

'Walk around and mingle.' The course director's words send me into a panic. I don't do walking around and mingling. In a wheelchair it's pretty nigh impossible.

This morning when asked to state along with everyone else what I brought to the course I said, 'Power'. It just came out. At this very moment, although I'm panicking, I also feel powerful. We have been asked to choose the people we want in our tutor groups. It feels important. I have chosen, but they don't know it yet. Delia because she looks fearless, but warm. She is also very talented. I love talent; I'm so drawn to it. Penny, who seems wise and fair, works with alcoholics, so there must be some links between us. Len, one of the only three men on the course, because he seems to want to enjoy himself. He works in a hospice; he seems real and very interesting. Rita would be my final choice, a woman obviously not afraid to speak her mind. She seems very different from the others and I think she would confront me. Maybe we could learn a lot from each other.

But unlike everyone else, I must wait to see who will choose me, if anyone. Then a strange feeling comes over me, one that I haven't ever really allowed to happen before. I cannot control the situation, I have no choice. Will anyone come to me? This thing, this disability, forces me to accept, forces me not to take control. I need them to recognize me; I cannot rush to find acceptance. I cannot be the child who grabs the nearest person when the teacher says, 'Find a partner!'

I find myself surrounded by people. I am pleased, relieved, elated. So many people want to work with me. The first to speak is Len

'Can I be in your group,' he asks 'because you look like Julie Walters?'
It's been years since anyone said that to me. Then something breath-
taking happens. Among the people who are sitting down by me,
because they've chosen me are Delia, Penny and finally Rita saying,
'I don't think this group would be easy for me and because of this I'd
like to work with you'. I want to laugh and tell them I had already
chosen them. How did they know?

It occurred to me that this was a classic example of what Moreno
(1977) called 'tele'. I first encountered this concept several years
ago when my work in theatre included the experience of psychodrama. In psychodrama, the person who has opted to work on some
personal problem or issue (known as the 'protagonist' in the jargon)
chooses people (known as 'auxiliary egos') to play the role of significant others in the protagonist's story. Through 'tele' a protagonist
will sense which members of the group have the potential to play the
required role. It's a strange, two-way flow of feeling between people.
'Just knowing' is what Moreno calls 'tele'. I must have just known
that Len, Delia, Penny and Rita would choose me. They were to
become very important people to me, as indeed they still are.

'Are the transfers here?'

Miss Smith is definitely a virgin. She is shaped like a light bulb,
wears woollen cardigans and when she sits down I can see her long
knickers because she sits with her legs apart. I am a *transfer* from the
secondary modern school to the grammar school. She knows this. She
hates me, probably because I am young and the boys like me. I know
she hates me because she told me so.

> Transference is the unconscious shifting to the therapist by the client of
> feelings and fantasies, both positive and negative that are displacements
> from reactions to significant others in the client's past. (Corey, 1991,
> p. 163)

It was a long time before I realized whom my tutor reminded
me of. I have met a few people who have voices that are not their real
voices. It is interesting to consider why some people re-invent the
way they speak. There are the obvious, getting rid of an accent,
using a phone or an interview voice, or even adopting a counselling
voice. We may while working, adopt a tone or inflection to affirm
what the client is saying, or to show that we are taking very seriously
their pain. This is obviously very important and something that

perhaps is not considered enough in training. But this is very different from what may be described as an adopted or acted voice, which has nothing to do with genuine empathy or acceptance. It has a lot more to do with playing the part. It is superficial, not real, and any client who wants to will soon suss it out.

And so I go with my chosen group in those first two days to meet my tutor. I sense a lot of warmth and certainly knowledge and most of what she says resonates with me.

Yet I am at times overwhelmed with a desire to laugh I feel so uneasy. I don't believe in – any of it! I dare not admit these feelings to myself. I dare not ask where they come from. I just feel instead, I know I will need her help. Her voice rings in my ears. Now I know that voice. I have heard it before. 'I hate you', it says 'I don't want you in my class. You make me sick.'

My tutor expresses many wishes, one of them is to 'stay in role' I am very uncomfortable with this. I have been 'cared for' by people who were 'in role', and I have been beaten by them. When I needed her she stayed in role, in her own way, she beat me.

Now, three years later I would question whether I misunderstood my tutor's role. Perhaps mistakenly I thought we were there to support each other. I thought somehow that she could represent us, but we should have represented ourselves. I didn't realize that the struggle to get to the university had left me needing affirmation that I was wanted there. I didn't get it. I didn't answer her phone calls; it was too late, I was too angry.

She wasn't Miss Smith of course. I know this, but I felt I had been here before. She guided us well academically and, perhaps, had I stayed on the course, she and I might have had a better relationship. What I was feeling was, of course, my own stuff and perhaps in time I would have been able to express my feelings. As it was, I tried to be the *good* student, the *good* pupil, but I was too old for those games now. I lacked the courage to confront her with my feelings. The way the group was run didn't open any doors in that direction for me. I was told to 'shut up' by her, so I did.

An arrangement has been made at the end of day two for first and second year students to get together for a glass of wine and a chat. We make our way to the meeting room. I go with my chosen tutor group when my friend, one of the lecturers comes back to tell me I can't get into the space. It isn't accessible. My group refuses to go and insist on staying with me.

I am amazed after all that has happened; this first important meeting is denied me. I feel foolish, embarrassed, I have become a problem, I want to go away, I want to be the same, equal. They have forgotten me. I am not equal, and I cause problems. I don't have special needs. No one has special needs – just needs, such as water, electricity, money. We all have needs, they only become special when they are about to be denied.

Are you **D**eaf?
Are you bl**I**nd?
Can't you **S**ee me?
Can't you he**A**r me?
And do you **B**lame
my disab**I**lity
for your **L**ack
of **I**nsight
for your shor**T**comings?
Do **Y**ou?
Jenni Meredith (1994)

There is no apology from the director of the course. In fact, he doesn't seem to know I'm here!

As Gregor Samsa awoke one morning from uneasy dreams, he found himself transformed in his bed into a gigantic insect. He was lying on his hard, as it were armour-plated, back and when he lifted his head a little he could see his domelike brown belly divided into stiff arched segments on top of which the bed quilt could hardly keep in position and was about to slide off completely. His numerous legs, which were pitifully thin compared to the rest of his bulk, waved helplessly before his eyes.

What has happened to me? he thought. It was no dream
Franz Kafka (1971, p. 9)

Dying isn't like the movies. Almost dying, or waiting to die on a daily basis, is quite farcical. Things go wrong. The machine stops. My eye – the one that works, that is – frantically looks for someone to save me. A nurse comes to my bed. 'We're going to lose her', she says calmly, given the situation.

You feel the breath leaving your body, your eyes fill with tears, tears for the baby you will never see again. Where's the bloody machine? Isn't someone going to fix it, to give me back my breath? The faces round the bed are stiff. I am fading. There is a certain peace in this; I want to laugh. Is this it then? Death. Is this how you do it? I'm not ready; I don't want to go, not for a mistake, maybe for the disease, but not this.

And I know they will never know, even my child will never know. He will forget me. They will tell him I didn't make it. They will never know they messed up, and they nearly killed me again.

Now the noise of the machine, the noise that keeps you awake when the drugs have gone, seems like a saviour. Oh God, where is my breath? A nurse inspired rushes and fiddles with my neck. There is a sudden gush of air and I am back. Back, alive, here again – in this nightmare. Nevertheless, I am here.

I hate hospitals. I've always hated them; they make me feel ill. It still haunts me even as I write this, the sound of the machine breathing for me, the monitors, the needles, the drips, all plumbed into me like having a canteen of cutlery attached. When they move me, it rips my skin, the leads tangle and burn against my flesh. I am part of the machine, but it does not always work. It does not tell them when I'm choking when huge bubbles of spit come down my nose, when my tracheotomy needs adjusting.

I had woken like Gregor; I had become an insect. No legs, no arms, my body freezes, only one ridiculous eye works. I wanted to laugh, I am hysterical, terrified. It's very rare they tell me, the Guillain-Barre syndrome. Only one in fifty thousand will ever get it, even in its mildest form. Fancy that! I am an enigma, a curious specimen.

This is a journey I travel alone. Until now, I have not really understood what 'alone' meant – the alone that few of us experience. I cannot speak. For four months I live entirely in my head. I watch my husband afraid to show me his fear, afraid to show me his love. It's not like the movies. He cleans me, washes me, wipes the shit from me. Now suddenly he is partner, mother, father, nurse, advocate. Now afraid, then angry at my bruises, he looks for an explanation. I cannot tell him, I cannot speak. We spell out the alphabet with my working eye. He guesses the letters, with ridiculous results! My arms ache for my baby and then I forget him, this separation could kill me. I must forget for now so that I can live for him later.

I was on my journey; I was becoming a new physical me. I was the 'meat' in intensive care. It took six people to move me and because of the pain of being touched they lifted me with a sheet. They took the body, my body. 'You take the legs', they said. Few of them knew who I was. A year in hospital, four and a half months in intensive care this is my poem for the staff there.

Intensive scare
This is no place for the sick.
Sick at heart.
Sick to their stomachs.
Sick of living.
No!
This is a place where
Machines live
Gasping their last breath
For someone
(To Harry who didn't make it and for baby Michael who fought them
and did.)

I'm in my personal development group, and I have just told them my story, the story you have just read. They asked me how I came to be disabled, why I can't walk and why my hands don't work. They sit horrified when I finish. They are angry. Is it worth it I wonder? Was it worth telling them? Is it worth telling you? Some things are beyond our grasp; perhaps this will be one of them.

I sense their emptiness. A silence ensues, another of those endless silences when no one knows what to say or what to do. I'm not ready to move on. I had high hopes of the work we might do in this group. I'm disappointed. No one seems prepared to share how they feel in this group. The 'meaningful' silences make my head ache. I am full of my pain for my story, my face is tight, I can't speak. The lecturer eventually breaks the silence, thanks me and we move on. And so the weeks go by.

I feel like sending this memo to all staff:

Guess what! I spoke to Andrew recently. Remember him? He's disabled like me. Nice guy, really hunky. What a laugh! Remember Andrew and me battling our way down a ramp where some idiots had chained their bikes to the railing. There's me in a wheelchair and Andrew, almost blind! Lucky for us along came the 'Cavalry', or the Director of the course, as he was more formally known. He rushed to help, confidently telling us how easy it is and not to worry. So comforting, these people with real power.

Andrew is still waiting to get his qualification sorted out. Some fool sent his work back with comments in pen and pencil all over it. What a pair! I can't get up the steps to the front of the library and Andrew isn't getting any of the help he needs with reading matter. Of course, we both know there's no money and, as people are always suggesting, surely we could find someone to help us. Who is this person?!! Please let us meet him/her.

Andrew would like me to say that if he had the choice again he would never have chosen this University. He doesn't feel that you really wanted us there, neither do I. Still, maybe someone reading this will insist that things improve. Hmm.

There is a view that our differences can be ignored because they are negative. By pretending they are not, then we can make like they don't exist, and maybe they will go away! But in rejecting my differences people reject me. How can I live with my differences if I forget them in order to fit it? It won't work. It only takes one stair to make all the difference to me. You can be sure the problem will be mine, not yours. I will be the one with the chip on my shoulder.

Change comes about when people strive to overcome their fears and take control over their own lives, when they allow their authenticity to exist, when they are prepared to stand and be counted. I did protest and let me be clear so did some of the students. It was generally not with the student body that I found lack of support, but with those in charge. I wanted to be a student, a counsellor, but instead I became a problem.

So how could things have been better for me? How can we begin to put things right? The answer seems to lie with an approach to training that I have used with my son and owes its roots to A. S. Neil, the founder of Summerhill School, Roland Meighan, John Davey and to the Parkway System (the school without walls) in Philadelphia.

I refer to the self-directed learning approach (SDL). SDL provides an important input into some counselling course. This is how it is described in Mary Charleton's book *Self-Directed Learning in Counsellor Training* (1996):

> Self-directed learning is a method of learning in which students set their own objectives and gain the knowledge and skills they require. Self-directed learning places the power and responsibility in the hands of the learner. It aims to give the learner as much control as possible over the what and the *how* of learning. The teacher or staff member becomes a facilitator who ensures that the conditions for effective learning exist. She watches over the process of learning and makes comments, which are intended to help the learner understand her way of working. The learner is expected to become aware of her personal and professional aims and to arrive at goals which support these aims. As the students learn about counselling they also learn to plan and to govern themselves as a community; they set up student-run workshops and other projects to support and

illuminate their learning; they produce a portfolio of work; they plan and set up a timetable based on needs and resources and they take part in individual and group supervision. They direct the learning and are closely involved in it. That involvement is personal and uses their senses, imagination, emotions and intellect. (pp. 4–5)

The diploma/MA course I undertook had many of the elements described above. However, I had anticipated that there would be much more. My training in theatre work and my own experience of productive counselling had been self-directed, and this influenced my expectation of the course. Within SDL issues of race, gender, (dis)ability would all have been given airtime and would have been part of the design of the course as Charleton (1996) points out:

> Staff and students should continually be searching for ways in which equal opportunities can be increased. The main ways in which staff do this is by helping the students to be clear about their personal learning needs and encouraging them to continually monitor whether or not these are being met. Staff constantly try to make sure that students are not being ignored or excluded. They do this in formal ways through tutorials and through being informally available and accessible to individuals. (p. 44)

I wished for space to be given to address issues, perhaps because the basic issue of access kept rearing its irritating head for me. My need for a forum in which to raise problems became more pronounced. Of course, no-one stopped me raising problems, but there is an important difference between a course where the raising of issues is built into the training and from which everyone learns and one in which the only place for raising issues is between sessions, during the lunch time or over coffee with a few willing listeners.

The most enjoyable times for me during my brief stay on the course were the workshop groups. This was where I really experienced SDL – an exchange of ideas, lots of learning and wonderfully stimulating discussion. We, the students, made decisions, made demands, tried to care about each other and learned in a self-directed way. It was during these occasions that we confronted our fears and explored the nature of fear.

We did not look to be nannied. Sometimes it is only when groups of people are asked to forget their fears and support others that the means for change becomes available. I believe that one of the most useful questions a counsellor can ask a client is, 'What is it you're afraid of?'

One last sad incident led me to believe that the support I needed was not there for me. As far as I was concerned, this was the LAST STRAW:

I was in the coffee bar with Penny and Merv, my husband. It was lunchtime, December. I enjoyed being with everyone at lunchtime. It would have been good to have been without Merv, but going to the loo was still a problem, despite the physical amenities which had been installed. I wasn't brave enough to risk it myself; I was too scared of falling. One of the students, with great respect, offered to help me, but I couldn't bring myself to accept.

The coffee bar was always packed at break times and since I couldn't reach the counter or open the packaging around the sandwiches, I brought my own lunch from home, in an attempt to maintain a degree of independence. I bought tea from the counter that someone else carried for me. At about 1.45 pm a member of the servery staff approached me and pointed out that people were not allowed to eat their own food in the servery. I informed her that since I couldn't reach the counter, hold money or open sandwiches, it wasn't possible for me to use the facilities available. She pointed out that I could get help if I asked.

The world can look very scary from wheelchair height. Since at coffee break and many lunch times I had found myself faced with a sea of legs and the prospect of being scalded by hot drinks, soup etc., I had come to the conclusion that bellowing for help amid the masses was not the wisest way of going about things. Besides which, it would deprive me of my independence.

Thus what I regarded as a small and insignificant incident was rapidly turning into an ugly scene. Merv and I were told we would be removed by security officers and not allowed back. I saw before me a large window through which I could very happily have thrown my cup. It was as if five years of abuse had come to a head. For Merv it reminded him of his helplessness at leaving me with nurses he didn't trust. Except, on this occasion he could stay and fight. All that unfinished business from the past came surging forward. Merv was white with anger and ready to protect me. Penny and I managed to persuade him to leave. He went, upset, and as he had done on many occasions before, sat in his car, alone.

As for me, I arrived with the valiant Penny (to whom I shall always be grateful) at our tutorial in need of much support. I have learnt in the past seven years to hold back tears and to put on a brave face. But on this occasion I shook from head to foot. I could hardly speak. But gradually the silly, sorry tale came out mostly from Penny. My tutor group was very upset and angry. I had needed understanding in the servery but what I got was abuse. I couldn't fight this alone. Somewhere deep inside me was an awareness that I had made a decision. I had had enough.

On a course that makes full use of SDL, sometimes the tutors must take on the hierarchy. My tutor, reminding me very much of the Queen, stated that the incident was very serious and that she would bring it to the attention of the staff group. Only one lecturer came to find me to offer support. The following week, without a trace of emotion, my tutor informed us that the staff had discussed the incident and had come to the conclusion that the problem was a student one and that it should not therefore involve any of them.

So there it was, another fight. It was up to me to see whose support I would get. Would any of my student colleagues take the risk, would they get their hands dirty for me? I had a strong sense that without the firm backing of the lecturing body they wouldn't be there for me. I guess I was too tired and too hurt to find out. Dear Delia and Penny stuck by me at lunch times after that. We ate together in one of the classrooms. I made myself ask them to stay with me because I felt I had nowhere else to go which was accessible. This they did and admonished me from my fear of asking. It may seem small and petty, but I hated it. I hated that I had lost the choice and I hated that they may have done too.

Although I returned after Christmas, mentally it was at this moment I left. I caused problems, people felt uneasy, or it seemed to me that they did. I was convinced that the people who could have effected change chose not to. Well, I still had a choice! So I left in February. If I learned anything from my attempt to do the diploma/MA it is that I can walk (or wheel) away. I can face my fear and say, 'No. It's not for me'.

Yes, I needed support. I needed time to learn to be the new me, to live in this strange place in which I found myself. I had to leave the course to do this. I'm still fearful and I'm still trying to learn to say no. My support comes from many places, but mainly from Merv, my partner, who probably is a saint. He is and was 'always on my mind', which is why we stay together. With him I fit, I am an equal. My support also comes from my son, Alf, whom I lost for a year and who at the age of two took the trouble to find me again, despite the many people who were in his way. Thank you, sweetheart.

I hope this brief piece of writing gives you, the reader, opportunity to question, to laugh, to reflect and, perhaps, face your fears.

> All this he saw, for one moment breathless and intense, vivid on the morning sky; and still, as he looked, he lived; and still, as he lived, he wondered.
> 'Rat!' he found breath to whisper, shaking. 'Are you afraid?'
> 'Afraid?' murmured the Rat, his eyes shining with unutterable love.
> 'Afraid! Of *Him*? O, never, never! And yet – and yet – O, Mole I am afraid!'
>
> Kenneth Grahame (1997, p. 100)

Author's note
The students referred to in this chapter are real people; the names are fictitious.

References

Beckett, S. (1958) *Endgame*, London: Faber & Faber.

Bell, M. H. (1997) *Whistle Down the Wind*, London: Sceptre.

Brookes, P. (1972) *The Empty Space*, Harmondsworth: Penguin.

Charleton, M. (1996) *Self-Directed Learning in Counsellor Training*, London: Cassell.

Corey, G. (1991) *Theory and Practice of Counseling and Psychotherapy*, 4th edn, Pacific Grove, CA: Brooks/Cole, p. 163.

Grahame, K. (1997) *The Wind in the Willows*, London: Pavillion Classics.

Kafka, F. (1971) *Metamorphosis and Other Stories*, Harmondsworth: Penguin.

McGough, R. (1976) 'First Day at School', in *Strictly Private*, Harmondsworth: Penguin.

Meredith, J. (1994) 'Disability', in K. Lios (ed.), *Mustn't Grumble – Writings by Disabled Women*, London: Women's Press.

Moreno, J. L. (1977) cited in P. Holmes and M. Karp (eds) (1991) *Psychodrama Inspiration and Technique*, London: Tavistock/Routledge.

Orwell, G. (1945) *Animal Farm: a fairy story*, London: Secker and Warburg.

Sondheim, S. (distributed by IMP 1985) *Send in the Clowns*, London: Chappell Music.

9

A Weird and Complex Business

Pat Garrigan

Readers may wonder whether the title of this chapter is the author's appraisal of the work of a counsellor! Pat Garrigan starts with the end of her story by stating unequivocally that after three years of training and a master's degree she arrived at the decision that counselling was not for her. She traces the sequence of events in her life, the happy times and the sad times, the insight and the disillusionment that led up to her decision. Her purpose in telling this story is that others contemplating training might ask whether becoming a counsellor is for them. She has some pertinent observations for trainers of counsellors as well, such as the importance of creating a sense of community within the student group and the danger of colluding in the maintaining of a safe and cosy environment. The author gives a clear account of the emotional cost of counselling.

When I was invited to contribute a chapter to a book about the experience of counsellor training, my immediate response was a paradoxical one. I was both excited and daunted by the prospect. The thought that my story, which ended with the decision not to become a counsellor, might be of interest to others was exciting. But it was also daunting, because counsellor training taught me to recognize my 'self-doubt' that all too easily could cast a shadow over my life. I recall moments of inspiration interspersed among periods of despair, as I toiled over essays and, in the final year, a dissertation. Words uttered all too often during times of doubt were 'never again'. Yet here I am about to recollect, reflect and relive the training experience. During three years of training, I learned a great deal about myself, my priorities, and about the weird and complex business of counselling. And although I became disillusioned with counselling, as a way forward in my career, being a trainee was a significant part of an important period in my life.

What, if anything, can I say about the weird and complex world of counselling to inform those about to embark on a course, or those already involved in the roller coaster ride of training. As someone who became disillusioned with counselling, what can I add to the discussion? An individual's journey to counsellor training and sub-sequent sojourn through the years of training stand as a unique testimony to their learning experience. Below are thoughts about parts of my own journey and perhaps, in telling my tale, others may recognize familiar landmarks, or appreciate better their own path. I begin at the end, as finishing training, and the ritual of the gradua-tion ceremony, became the light at the end of a very long and ardu-ous tunnel.

Ending and beginning – gowns and tarot cards

During my congregation I experienced a range of different emotions. I was anxious, apprehensive, excited, proud, nervous, reflective, dis-appointed, impressed, sad and happy. As I gathered alongside my fellow course survivors, I wondered about those who were not with us, casualties, perhaps, of the academic process.

Looking up into the dry, grey December morning, flanked by buildings that served to remind anyone present of the historical gran-deur of the setting, and surrounded by people in academic gowns, self-conscious myself in academic dress, I mused to myself that tast-ing, experiencing, being part of this present moment, had been the inspiration of my last year of study. I had longed for this moment, as I had toiled over the task of writing up my research dissertation; a dissertation that ironically was a personal reflection on why I no longer wished to counsel. During the seemingly endless moments of 'writer's block', of wanting to 'pack it all in', and feeling 'I can't do this', the thought of this very moment had kept me going. I also recalled the events that led up to my application for the course.

Leading up to the course, I had been putting a lot of serious thought into the next step in my personal development. I had com-pleted a counselling skills course and had recently helped facilitate on a similar course. However, the final decision to apply for an MA in counselling occurred in a more flippant vein. After initially requesting the course information, the application form had lain uncompleted, while I pondered and deliberated. Why do this particular course? Could I cope? I was concerned with both the standard of study and the time commitment, and also whether I could afford the course fees.

Then one late, lazy August day, I was with friends at a summer festival where a woman was reading tarot cards. Out of fun, I had my cards read. One of the cards predicted success in study, and I remember turning to my friends and saying, 'Well, I'll have to fill that application form in now!' Whether it was the final spur I needed, I don't know, but on returning home I completed a late application. Within a matter of weeks I was interviewed and began the course.

What I remember most vividly about this process was that I never previously had any serious thoughts about wanting to change my career as a career advisor and become a full-time counsellor. Rather I hoped the course would enhance my counselling skills and provide an environment for further personal development. In retrospect, the fact that my decision to apply turned on something so seemingly irrational as a superstitious prediction of success contrasts with the immense sense of both achievement and relief I felt on graduation day. What the fortune teller did not predict was how seriously I would question my motivation to train as a counsellor. It is the major theme of this chapter.

The process begins – the first year

The course was part time, two years to reach diploma level and a further year to gain an MA. The first two years were a combination of theory, learning counselling skills and personal development. The final year consisted of a course in research methodology and the completion of a research project.

I suppose I began the course with a rather naive attitude towards counselling. I was slightly daunted by the fact that some of the other course participants were full-time counsellors, and imagined they were following the course, not so much to learn as to gain a 'piece of paper', which acknowledged their expertise. Still others were involved in voluntary counselling, or jobs that included a lot of client contact where counselling was one of the tools they employed. I was impressed at the breadth of knowledge of my fellow students, and the range of different personalities. I felt exited and enthusiastic, and confident that we could learn a great deal from one another. I enjoyed the whole adventure of learning, and each week looked forward to the course meetings. The theoretical input was stimulating and prompted a great deal of reflection. I enjoyed the balance of different teaching and learning styles and taking part in experiential group activities.

Highlights

There had been many highlights during my three years training programme. One of my lasting memories will be of my small video group where counselling was practised. My most profound learning took place during the video group time; for example, experiencing, and coming to understand, 'unconditional positive regard' in a way that could never be captured in essays or peer assessment reports. Indeed, it is difficult to find words to describe exactly what took place within the learning environment of the small video group. We made mistakes, and stumbled and staggered through attempts to 'work with the client's frame of reference', 'use the relationship', 'respond to metaphor/imagery', or 'work reflectively in combination with challenge and immediacy'. This was the language of the course, and in skills training, I began to experience what it meant.

We had our moments, each individual demonstrating different styles and techniques, learning from each other, moaning about the course or the work, laughing with one another, gaining support, insights and healing along the way. More importantly, I felt, we were able to 'to be' ourselves in our video group. We were there for one another, masks off, open, genuine, honest and respectful to one another. It was perhaps like the intangible process of counselling itself.

Clients – the unstructured learning element

Counselling practice is the unstructured, unpredictable learning element of training. I learned a great deal from clients, and am grateful to the many people who became my clients during my training years. There were successes, failures, mistakes, tears, laughter; all part of relationships formed, lived through and then ended. I often wonder where those people are now, and how they look back on our time together.

One of the problems I faced was finding clients. Having a full-time job, my only opportunity to gain counselling experience was through a voluntary agency. I usually worked two nights a week, depending on client demand. Finding clients in this way was rather like being thrust into the engine room of learning, this was where it all happened. I never felt I saw the whole picture of a client's situation or had any indication of what kind of issues a client would present, nor what problems I would have to deal with. Other than supervision, I had no backup, and there was no referral system. In my first year I was hurled into the harsh work of clients' pain. I met people who were encountering physical or sexual abuse, mental illness, suicide, bereavement, or eating disorders. I do not think anything could have really prepared me for this. I needed these clients, yet, in the early months, I wished that some of their issues were less complicated and painful. They were indeed the unstructured, unpredictable and yet unmissable learning element of training.

With client work, came the stark recognition of my commitment to training. Unlike other elements of the course, they were not something I could choose to 'give a miss'. I began to feel the personal and emotional cost of counsellor training. There were times when I felt twinges of resentment as I travelled to see clients, of thinking – I hope that they appreciated what I am doing. I sometimes even hoped there would be a cancellation and I would not have to go. I wondered why I could never say 'no' to a request for counselling. Indeed, I felt I had a personal need to respond, a need which I reflected upon increasingly as I began to question my motivation to become a counsellor.

Stresses and strains

I sometimes felt that I had taken on too much, and by the end of the second year I felt I wanted a break. I had had enough. There is an emotional cost to counselling that I had not realized at the outset of the course. I often felt that my life was a balancing act between meeting the demands of my personal life, full-time work and voluntary counselling work. My first thoughts about no longer wishing to counsel were: 'I am tired ... I don't want to do it anymore ... I have enough people in my life'.

Much has been written about the stresses and strains of counselling (Brady, Healy, Norcross and Guy, 1995; Kottler, 1986; Guy,

1987) and I recognize myself in much that has been described. For example:

> The stresses of a counsellor in training can be viewed as a multiple demand difficulty. Where the demands of the training course requirements themselves are combined with occupational demands, be they related or not, and the demands of the counsellor's private life. (Jensen, 1995, p. 188)

Brady *et al.* (1995) describe how demands and events in a person's life can significantly interfere with one's situation and life events can cause considerable distress in the therapist's own inner world.

My own experience of a significantly distressing life event occurred towards the end of the first year of training and vibrated throughout the second year of the course. This was the death of my beautiful and precious five-day-old baby granddaughter. This was not some sudden tragic event, but rather an inevitable consequence of a condition diagnosed at a routine ante-natal scan, several months prior to her death. As a family, and primarily for my daughter and son-in-law, looking forward, and anticipating, the time of birth was tinged with a unique kind of sadness, because we did not know how long she would live. We also knew that soon after birth, death would follow. We had no idea how long we would have, which made every moment we did have something very special indeed.

I learned about my daughter's fateful news shortly before I was due to leave on an alternative holiday/personal-development course, not long before the end of the first year of the course. The scan indicated that the baby had a serious heart condition, later diagnosed as hypoplastic left heart syndrome.

I left for my holiday/personal development course with very mixed emotions: guilty about going away; and a sense of impotence that, even if I were at home, there was very little I could do. I also harboured hopes that perhaps the hospital had got it wrong. Going away at that time was like entering an alternative universe.

The holiday was another learning experience for me. It was a week in which to explore personal myths. I held the sadness about my daughter close to me, in a kind of sacred solitude, while at the same time I marvelled at the skills of the course leader, and the process that can take a group of strangers and build them into a community.

On returning to the counselling course, I felt sadness that as a group of students we had somehow not quite managed to achieve this sense of community. In front of the large group I shared my sad news, and in all honesty, felt slightly let down by the response. Perhaps I was expecting too much. This feeling was not something related to individuals, because from individuals I found a great deal of support over the coming months, but something related to the healing power or the support that one can receive from a group of people. Somehow, in the dynamics of a large group, I was left with the impression that some expressions of vulnerability were not welcome.

The second year of study saw my whole philosophy on life tested and honed in a very dramatic way. I was, and still am, intensely proud of my daughter. I think she had a tremendous burden to carry, and somehow in the five days that her daughter lived we, as a whole family, entered into the great mystery of life and death. I watched my daughter's suffering, and learned that choosing an easy option is a delusion; there are no quick solutions or instant remedies. Suffering cannot be avoided. Sometimes, we just have to go through the pain and, although the pain is harsh and cuts a deep groove, it instils in us a capacity to appreciate suffering in others and an ability to appreciate the joy and wonder of life.

When dealing with clients I was amazed at my ability to lay aside my own concerns and sadness and enter with ease into the drama of their world. Perhaps this was a temporary escape, but within the climate of my own pain, somehow my confidence and professional competence as a counsellor grew.

Disillusionment sets in

Towards the end of the second year, I began to question seriously whether counselling was for me. I began to feel disillusioned about counselling as I entered the research year. I missed the regular contact with fellow students and the support of structured group work. I missed the practical training, feeling there was so much still to learn. I experienced 'anxious loneliness' (Skovholt and Ronnestad, 1995). I had underestimated the stresses I had been exposed to during my training and realized that the disillusionment I was feeling had been brought on by a complexity of different factors all coming together at a particular time in my life.

There were also times when I felt frustrated and disappointed. More often than not, this was during time set aside for personal development group work. One of my reasons for wanting to enter counsellor training was the prospect of engaging in the challenge of a personal development group. However, this aspect of the course never quite lived up to my expectations. It was not until the third year, when writing my dissertation, that I found the challenge I had been looking for.

Missed opportunities

While writing the dissertation I had plenty of time to reflect on missed learning opportunities, especially those that could have occurred in the personal development group. I also wondered how much of this was my own fault. Had I missed out on opportunities to gain greater insights offered during personal development time? The BAC *Code of Ethics for Practice Trainers* states that 'trainers have a responsibility to encourage and facilitate the self-development of trainees . . .' (BAC, 1995). This is about providing a space and time for self-development, self-reflection and self-awareness.

My personal development group had been a comfortable place to be, but had lacked an 'element of challenge', to use a phrase of Carl Rogers (Rogers, 1971). On reflection, I feel that perhaps everyone, including myself, colluded to maintain a safe and cosy atmosphere, not wishing to create waves and stir things up. Most of all, an atmosphere that reflected a lack of commitment pervaded this allotted time. For example, this would be the part of the course schedule more likely to be shortened or dropped if the timetable was running late. I also felt there was a lack of commitment from some members of the personal development group, reflected in lateness, absences, and even declarations that they felt it was a waste of time. This established some kind of benchmark of trust that was difficult to move beyond, so that I thought: 'Why make myself vulnerable, when I know you would rather not be here!' I think this was partly because each individual held a different understanding about the purpose of the group.

My expectations of personal development within group work were similar to Dryden's description of client change, which:

> . . . by its very nature, involves clients moving away from familiarity into areas where they are bound to experience uncomfortable feelings which they need to tolerate or 'stay with' if they are to move on. (Dryden, 1992, p. 41)

I know I had found this depth of challenge in other courses I had attended, particularly week-long residential courses. Having experienced this element of challenge, I wanted more, and this was part of the reason to undertake counsellor training. I felt I did have a commitment to personal development work, hence I had attended a variety of group work courses, which encouraged self-reflection.

> The overall aims of group work have to do with personal growth and development, encouraging enquiry into personal behavioural style and providing participants with an opportunity to gain insights and awareness of the impact of their own behaviours and how they are viewed by others, together with an increasing sensitivity to what others are feeling. (Taylor, 1981, pp. 137–139)

One of the key lessons I have learned is that this element is one of the most important aspects of counsellor training, and that, yes, it needs to be effectively organized with trainees understanding the purpose of the group, but also with a commitment from trainees to each other's development. It is rather like being both a client and counsellor to one another.

Understanding my motivation

As already mentioned, embarking on the MA in counselling was not because of some desire to change career, but rather an expression of a deeper motivational process begun many years ago when I received counselling myself. At the time I never quite understood what this motivational process was about. Looking back over the years of training, however, especially the research year, I have gained a clarity that feels personally satisfying, I now know why I did the course. I also feel slightly sad that this was not something I could explore with the help of my fellow students.

I wanted also to enhance my skills as a careers adviser. I was dealing increasingly with people with personal and work related problems and I wanted to help. Any thoughts I may have harboured about being a full-time counsellor were placed firmly to the back of my mind. Rather, I wanted to enhance my skills in order to improve my effectiveness as a careers adviser and to engage in the personal development that involvement in counselling training demands, and hence to be enabled:

to carry out their work with greater integrity and self-profession; they do not feel they are under siege by totally mysterious forces all the time. Neither do they feel that they must completely solve all the problems of those who come to see them. These paraprofessional counsellors can be highly skilled at assisting persons to take greater responsibility for them . . . The insights into themselves that they develop are also important and enable themselves to understand their own investment in their work with others. (Kennedy and Charles, 1990, p. 18)

Understanding my own investment and personal motivation became key concerns. In Kennedy and Charles' (1990) book there is a section entitled 'Hard-bought Wisdom', and I find many similarities here with my awareness into my own personal motivation. This was to do with being good and doing well, to want approval and appreciation.

I wanted to 'do well' and to be a good counsellor, not only for the client's sake, but also in academic terms, and I found that I constantly compared myself to others' performances. In Skovholt and Ronnestad's (1995) *The Evolving Professional Self*, there is a description of the 'anxiety of academic performance'. I totally recognized myself in their outline of the Central Task of the Transition Stage of Counsellor development. I was aware of the requirements of the course to take on board various techniques and theories and different ways of working, and of faceless external examiners who impose some of these academic pressures. I was also conscious of adhering to a code of ethics as laid down by the BAC. I had some difficulty with the issue of boundaries, clinging, perhaps naively, to simplistic ideas about how the process of counselling works when dealing with 'simple humanity that is considered too ordinary to be impressive' (Kennedy and Charles, 1990, p. 38). After three years of training, I still apply the notion of friendship to counselling, believing that ' this act of sympathetic friendship is one of the keys to the success of helping', and that 'if friendship is simple, and helping is like friendship, then this process is simple' (Skovholt and Ronnestad, p. 20).

I also felt the pressures of being 'forced into the framework of a polished performance' (Kennedy and Charles, 1990, p. 38) not so much by my tutors, but partly by the requirements of the course and my own desire to 'do well'. Understanding this desire, this need, and my underpinning personal motivation, were the major insights gained from counsellor training, and part of the reason why I decided being a full-time counsellor was not the career for me.

I began to place this examination of my motives in a wider context, and reflected on the profound influences in my life that culminated in counsellor training.

> Motivation is inextricably bound up with the wholeness of the person, with one's direction of movement, with one's struggles to authenticate oneself. (Friedman, 1992, p. 162)

If I had not decided to research my own personal motivation in such depth, I would never have gained the insights into the reasons for wanting to enter counselling in the first place and know the complex reasons behind why I became disillusioned.

Wheels that turn

I have my own story to tell, all kinds of events to describe, a history of who I am to understand, made up of my upbringing, education, religion, the influence of the many people who nurtured and influenced me. An important part of my story is the experience of being counselled. I have experienced two very different approaches as a client; both had a profound affect. After surviving the pain of divorce and emerging a much stronger person, there was a need in me to continue to learn from experience, and hopefully to grow more fully as a human being. It was movement towards self-actualization.

> We are speaking of the tendency of the organism to move in the direction of maturation . . . This involves self-actualization . . . It moves in the direction of limited expansion through growth, expansion through extending itself . . . It moves in the direction of greater independence or self-responsibility . . . and away from heteronymous control, or control by external forces. (Rogers, 1951, p. 488)

I discovered that 'basic needs can be fulfilled only by and through other human beings' and a self-actualizing person is often involved 'in a cause outside . . . themselves . . . some calling or vocation in the old sense' (Friedman, 1992, p. 16).

With the benefit of study, I came to understand that this drive to self-actualize had been hindered by negative influences in my life. I carried a legacy of never feeling quite good enough, I was always falling short, constantly aware of the gulf between where I was and what I was aspiring to become. When I engaged in counselling as a client and in subsequently taking up counsellor training, I found I was less harsh on myself and more accepting of my imperfections. Therefore, I was able to move away from negative influences, and found an alternative route by which to expand and grow as a person, and acquire a more healthy view of myself.

So I learned about my personal motivation. It reflected a need for personal development, a need to engage in meaningful exchanges with others, encounters where I felt I was touching the soul of another human being. I had found these encounters in personal development courses and when counselling clients. So I learned I was fulfilling a need in me through a cause outside myself, which involved helping other people. As Scott Peck writes:

> The truth is that we rarely do anything without some gain or benefit to ourselves, however small or subtle. (1997, p. 143)

I had found an outlet to 'be good . . . to do well . . . to win approval or appreciation . . . and help others'. Every time I felt tired and wanted to say 'no' but couldn't, even when I was busy, I was fulfilling this need in me. This need fulfilled some image of a person who denies her own needs for the sake of others, and who would hopefully, somehow, win approval. If I hadn't embarked on writing a personal piece of research for my dissertation year I would never have looked at my own personal motivation in any depth, believing, instead, that my reasons for counselling were totally 'altruistic', with no thought that I might be doing something for myself at the same time.

However, at the start of my third year, wheels began to turn when I took on a new client. This new counselling relationship was difficult for a number of reasons; one being that I didn't really think counselling was what the client needed. A more appropriate helping strategy would have been a befriending, or involvement with an ongoing support service. However, another reason was that I did not feel inclined to make all the effort. I questioned myself 'Why do it, do you really *need* to be doing this?' The topic of my dissertation was born.

The pennies really drop!

I found the essential challenge I was looking for through the discipline of writing an academic piece of work. Using a heuristic research methodology, an approach not unlike learning in a counselling relationship, I endeavoured to reflect on why I no longer wished to counsel.

Although the training years were difficult in terms of time, I am pleased I made the sacrifice. There has been a personal and emotional cost, but I learned some valuable lessons along the way. One of these lessons is something that Scott Peck (1997) writes about, that is the difference between insisting that we always feel good about ourselves, which he calls 'narcissistic' and insisting that we regard ourselves as important or valuable, which he calls 'healthy self-love'.

Therefore, I feel it is okay to say counselling is not for me, I have had enough ... certainly for now. It is time to take care of myself. I have learned that I really do not need to do this. Who knows – I may return to counselling, and if I do I hope I will remember what I have learned, and to walk with more confidence the tightrope that is the paradox of our existence:

> We are called upon to realise ourselves, yet to aim directly at so doing is always self-defeating. (Friedman, 1992, p. 17)

The closing words of my dissertation read:

> For those embarking on counsellor training, I would say: 'Don't underestimate the stresses and confusions that can arise during training. Make time for yourself, take care of yourself, share your anxieties, arrange for good supervision and pay attention to your learning process'.

I would also add:-

> *Value your personal development time.*

References

BAC (1995) *Code of Ethics and Practice for Trainers*, Rugby: British Association for Counselling, para. A1.4.

Brady, J. L., Healy, G. C., Norcross, J. C. and Guy, J. D. (1995) 'Stress in counsellors: an integrative research review', in W. Dryden (ed.), *Stresses of Counselling in Action*, London: Sage.

Dryden, W. (ed.) (1992) *Hard-earned Lessons from Counselling in Action*, London: Sage, p. 41.

Friedman, M. (1992) *Dialogue and the Human Image: Beyond Humanistic Psychology*, Newbury Park, CA: Sage.

Guy, J. D. (1987) *The Personal Life of the Psychotherapist*, New York: Wiley.

Jensen, K. H. (1995) 'The stresses of counsellors in training', in W. Dryden (ed.) (1995) *The Stresses of Counselling in Action*, London: Sage, p. 188.

Kennedy, E. and Charles, S. C. (1990) *On Becoming a Counsellor: A Basic Guide for Non-Professional Counsellors*, Dublin: Gill & Macmillan.

Kottler, J. A. (1986) *On Being a Therapist*, San Francisco: Jossey-Bass.

Peck, M. S. (1997) *The Road Less Travelled and Beyond: Spiritual Growth in an Age of Anxiety*, London: Rider.

Rogers, C. R. (1951) *Client-Centered Therapy: Its Current Practice, Implications and Theory*, Boston: Houghton Mifflin, p. 488.

Rogers, C. R. (1971) *Carl Rogers on Encounter Groups*, London: Penguin.

Skovholt, T. and Ronnestad, M. H. (1995) *The Evolving Professional Self: Stages and Themes in Therapist and Counsellor Development*, Chichester: Wiley.

Taylor, B. (1981) 'Experiential learning a framework for group skills. Leeds: Oasis Communication', in J. Irving and D. Williams *The Role of Group Work in Counsellor Training*, Counselling, 7(2), 137–139.

10

One Training Voice: Reflecting on the Echoes

Rhona Fear

This chapter is written by an experienced counsellor who looks back over the years since she first put herself forward for counselling training and reflects on the milestones, or 'critical incidents', which have marked her journey from being a trainee counsellor with Relate, to becoming a counsellor in private practice in Worcestershire. The importance of working out one's personal philosophy of life and finding a theoretical orientation that will reflect this belief system is given careful consideration. Rhona Fear looks at the positives and the negatives of training to be a counsellor: the effects on family and friends, as well as the effects on oneself. The place of personal therapy is thoughtfully examined.

It is some years since I completed my second major experience of counselling training. Thinking about writing a chapter for this book, and then writing it, has been therapeutic. It has given me with the opportunity to reflect upon the high spots, the low spots, the pain and the tears, the unforgettable moments of 'aha, now I understand', and the joys and disappointments of my own unique experience of counsellor training.

Each of us as counsellors undergoes a unique journey as we take the path of training. I have chosen a title for this chapter that suggests that in giving voice to my experience, in sharing my journey of personal and professional development, it may resonate or echo in some way with the experience of others. I have used concepts learned in training to make sense of what I have found valuable. Two ideas have been especially helpful: first, the idea of the 'critical incident';

and second, the idea of moving through different stages of professional and personal development.

My training has been undertaken in two distinct phases, each of which has fostered different aspects of my personal and professional growth, and each with its own traumas and rewards. My initial training took place within the containing and 'family' institution of Relate, National Marriage Guidance. There, learning took place in periodic pressurized episodes of formal classroom input coupled with the more informal learning gained from contact with clients and from individual and group supervision. I feel honoured and most fortunate to have received my initial counselling training from an organization that manages the interweaving of theory and practice so well. This memory, however, includes my woeful and heartfelt attempts to explain to my first supervisor how very inadequately prepared I felt to start seeing my first clients!

The training with Relate was followed by a 'moratorium' (Skovholt and Ronnestad, 1995) of several years. I used the time as a psychological sanctuary in which to take stock, to assimilate the learning and personal change which my journey into counselling had begun, and to reflect upon the way forward. Towards the end of that time, I made a conscious decision that I wanted the stimulus and wider perspective that only further training would provide. There followed the second stage of my training: a Masters degree programme. This took me to a new and different level of understanding and competence as a therapist.

Counsellor training involves a complex process of learning, for learning is not only recognized, encouraged and achieved at an academic level, but also at the personal level of development of reflective self-awareness. John McLeod (1993a) makes the extremely pertinent point that in most educational or training courses, be they in computing or plumbing, or even in psychology or nursing, the personal process is considered to be of little relevance except on occasions when it interferes with a student's performance. In the field of counselling and psychotherapy, however, the development of accurate, reflective self-awareness is absolutely central. It is part of learning holistically. From the day of the first contact with a client to the day one feels that one's professional and personal sense of identity have become integrated, learning to be a counsellor is a process of socialization. It is facilitated as much by the experience of being in a training group as by how the course is organized and what it contains.

My experience has led me to believe that the creation of an environment within which informal and formal learning blend together is at the heart of counsellor training.

Two themes ran through my learning as a trainee, and give shape to this chapter. First, there is a focus upon learning as an integrated process drawing upon both informal and formal learning opportunities. Second, I learned through a number of critical incidents. These were parts of the training experience that made a major impact on both my personal and professional selves. A critical incident is a 'transforming event' or 'developmental turning point' (Skovholt and McCarthy, 1988, pp. 69–110), and my critical incidents required a readiness and willingness to learn from the experience, to suffer both joy and heartache and to channel it into positive development.

Where I was at the beginning: psychically, emotionally, practically

At the age of forty, I found myself the mother of two daughters who were rapidly growing up and less in need of what I call 'all-day, everyday mothering'. For the past ten years I had taken the role of full-time wife and mother, and rewarding as that had been, I had an intuitive, not fully articulated, sense that it had left me with a loss of sense of identity. To use Ann Dickson's words, I was not 'a woman in her own right' (Dickson, 1982). The achievement of this has been a major task of my fifth decade. I was aware, therefore, of a need to develop and find a personal sense of purpose, particularly if I were to avoid an empty nest syndrome, and enable my daughters to separate from me without feelings of guilt that they were leaving Mum behind, unable to function alone. A vague awareness of this need to find something for myself had earlier led to my decision to retrain because I did not want to return to my earlier career in marketing and market research. Given my family commitments, I had undertaken a degree in social science through the Open University. My sense of competence and self-esteem grew in leaps and bounds when in 1990, I was awarded a first class honours degree. During the latter two years of my degree, I suffered a nagging and persistent feeling that I needed to find a career in which I could put my abilities to good, practical use. A concentrated search followed, in which I approached career consultants and read a lot of career literature. I wanted a career in which I could find a personal sense of achievement. I was blessed with the freedom to choose because I luckily had few serious financial constraints.

Enlightenment as to the way forward came suddenly and from a most unexpected source: a magazine article on a day in the life of three female counsellors. I was overtaken with a sense of excitement and exhilaration, even though it was two o'clock in the morning! This was what I wanted to do! However, in characteristic cautious style, I put my toe in the water by enrolling on a counselling skills course at a local college of further education. From the start, I was hooked! I had already made an application to Relate to train as a counsellor. I pursued my application with zeal and enthusiasm, and in September 1990 was selected as a trainee counsellor.

The initial training experience with Relate

Training with Relate was demanding. It overtook my life for its duration of two and a half years. Periods of intensive residential training were emotionally and physically exhausting. My own self-development was set in motion, by the formal parts of training, by awareness groups and by contact with clients from an early stage. I remember moments of insight gained in almost every case supervision group meeting, as we sat and discussed cases, careful of course to guard our clients' confidentiality. In individual supervision sessions, I learned to experience the reality of the normative, formative and restorative functions of supervision (Proctor, 1988). To me, it was as if I were a child led into a vast toyshop where I could constantly choose a new toy to stimulate and invigorate me.

The constant informal learning process was given a secure base by the formal, residential training modules, covering skills, theory and awareness. Skills practice in the form of role-play and video work produced embarrassment, much laughter and moments of 'aha'. Working experientially with peers, and letting vulnerabilities shine through, fostered interesting group dynamics that were explored in awareness groups. I learned to identify my typical role in a group: it is to stand slightly apart as a leader, a senior, even a mentor. On one occasion, I was forced to face one of my severest dreads, that of being ostracized by the group, in childish terms, 'sent to Coventry'. It was valuable personal learning, although traumatic. I faced the fear, worked through it and emerged the other side with some resolution as to how to deal with it effectively, and survive! Unexpected ways in which I was relating to clients were exposed when I discovered that one of my fellow trainees was struck, from the first moment of seeing me, with very strong child-mother transference. I now see Relate's theoretical orientation as eclectic, although at the time I had no understanding of theoretical issues that would have enabled me to label it thus. A lot of attention was given to psychodynamic theory. Cognitive and behavioural interventions were introduced to help couples achieve some relatively rapid and evident change that could foster motivation to work on their relationship. Systemic theory was also quite central. And person-centred skills were taught in order to enable the counsellor to develop a good, working therapeutic alliance.

However, it was psychodynamic theory that fascinated me. I could not consume enough literature on psychodynamic theory. I read, morning, noon and night. I found myself inexorably drawn towards Bowlby's attachment theory (Bowlby, 1979, 1988; Holmes, 1993), object relations theory (Cashden, 1998) and particularly towards the collusive defensive mechanism of projective identification (Ogden, 1992). Other books that became my 'bibles' were Malan's *Individual Psychotherapy and the Science of Psychodynamics* (1979), Casement's *On Learning from the Patient* (1985) and *Further Learning from the Patient* (1988), and Jacobs' *The Presenting Past* (1986). Here lay the roots of my fascination with long-term psychotherapy, although at this stage I had no conceptual understanding or awareness of the difference between relatively short-term counselling and psychotherapy. Eventually, some years later it was to cause the parting of the ways for me and Relate, but at this stage all I was aware of was of the toy box of psychodynamic literature beckoning me to come and play!

How did I emerge from this period of training? I feel that I emerged as a competent counsellor. It was a time of great enthusiasm and motivation. I remember only too well saying earnestly to my first supervisor as I took my final leave of her that I did so want to be a very good counsellor. Wisely, she remarked that I might do better if I relaxed a little. I took her warning to heart and resolved to use more of my authentic self and to be less skills oriented/aware. I was the novice who is more aware of her own competency and skills level than that of her clients (Stoltenberg and Delworth, 1987). And I felt competent only some of the time: in some situations I was confident, and in others I would be flung back to uncertainty as some new aspect of counselling reared its head. I remember my first (recognized) case of strong erotic transference that sent me scuttling for supervision and further reading.

Friends and family

The training changed another aspect of my life: namely, my relationship with people outside the counselling arena. Some of my friends viewed me with caution, as they feared that I would seek to counsel them, or even to psychoanalyse the most innocent of comments. It took some time to convince them that my professional self did not seek to impinge upon our personal relationships. Nevertheless, counsellor training did alter the nature of the relationships that I started to foster, and sadly, it also meant that some relationships foundered as I moved on in terms of personal development. Herein lies one of the negatives of both phases of my counselling training; as I have grown in terms of emotional literacy and capacity to establish relationships of intense emotional intimacy, I have found it increasingly difficult to engage in what I now term 'social intercourse'

My relationship with my two children has also been affected, sometimes for the better, sometimes for the worse. How many counsellors have been accused of 'Don't think you are with one of your clients now! I can see beyond the empathy to what you really want me to do'. The refrain, so familiar to parents of adolescents reluctant to be given advice, takes on an added meaning for counsellors who are perceived to spend their time imparting advice to needy clients. However, both my daughters also feel that at times I have been able to help them more ably simply because of my counselling abilities. Perhaps one of the hardest conflicts which close friends and family have grappled with as a result of my being a therapist is the sense of what I can best term 'nakedness'. It is the feeling that I can see through their 'outer garments' (their defence mechanisms) to their raw skin (their unconscious processes). As one of my friends puts it, somewhat tongue in cheek, 'I just hate talking to psychotherapists!' So I guess that there are negatives and positives, heartaches and losses as well as gains.

Moving on

As my formal training with Relate came to an end, I was offered and accepted a much-coveted role as a staff member of Relate. I took up a salaried position which offered me security of salary and working conditions. Perhaps as important for me was the recognition it afforded me as a professional. There followed a period where I gave all my devotion to Relate, working many more hours than my contract warranted. After 450 hours of counselling I became eligible to write my 'project' the successful completion of which earned me a nationally recognized certificate. The project is a case study of 5,000 words requiring the ability to marry counselling practice with understanding of theory. It proved to be my first 'critical incident'. In a style typical of my whole personal philosophy, I wanted to complete the project to the very best of my ability. I realized that my Relate training had left many theoretical gaps, a lack of understanding of how different theories compared and contrasted, and how the major theoretical orientations were underpinned by different philosophical traditions. I started once more to read, this time finding some tentative answers in John McLeod's *Introduction to Counselling* (1993b) and in Corey's seminal textbook (1991).

I became aware that my Relate training was not enough; I wanted to fill some of the gaps in my understanding of theory, in my understanding of therapy as a process. And I was hungry to grow in terms of self-awareness. So I decided to apply to undertake a masters degree in counselling. I made applications to two universities, and was delighted to be offered places by both. Being given the choice proved to be a second critical incident. Rationally and logistically, the choice I should have made given my geographical location and my theoretical leanings was obvious – the choice that offered training in psychodynamic counselling. However, for the first time in my life I decided to trust my gut instinct and to accept the offer of a place at the university further from home. I can honestly say that I have never looked back from trusting my intuitive self. The longer I live, the more I have learned to trust my 'gut reaction'.

My second experience of counselling training

The course answered my needs. It provided me with the training to develop my own integrative approach. From what I knew of the course and of the people who ran it, its commitment to integration mirrored my own journey towards a highly individualized chosen form of integrative practice. It represented for me the real purpose of counselling; that of working towards personal integration, so that clients achieve greater authenticity, a sense of peace and personal reconciliation, and the ability 'to integrate their own 'cut-off' parts of themselves, by daring to own the previously too-painful and distressing feelings' (Skovholt and Ronnestad, 1995, p. 16).

The masters programme consisted of a number of component parts. Each day began with a lecture on theoretical orientation; this was mainly a formal learning process, although sometimes experiential exercises proved to be most enlightening. While the input was of a formal learning nature, I welcomed the way in which some explanation of theory led, on occasions, to a huge 'aha' moment of insight about my own life.

Much learning was gained in workshops that formed the basis of the second part of each morning. These were presented sometimes by lecturers, and sometimes by students. They imparted knowledge (in the form of theoretical learning), skills and awareness. Essentially, they were run on a person-centred basis of student-led learning. This proved to be an interesting and insightful way to learn. Of particular note to me was the module on ethical issues. Each group of students led a seminar or workshop on a particular aspect of ethical concerns. Ethical issues within counselling are particularly enlightening if talked about in an atmosphere of debate, of open and frank discussion. I learned a great deal from preparing and presenting a seminar on the ethical issues concerned with dual relationships. This may have been a coincidence or it may have been synchronicity, as the issue of dual relationships arose in my client interactions at this very time. I experienced the counselling folk wisdom that 'you get the clients you need'. It was powerful learning, and has led to a consuming interest in ethical issues which has been invaluable ever since.

Tutorials formed the third part of the day. Here was the opportunity to practice skills, discuss academic concerns, and develop greater awareness of group dynamics. I found it almost incomprehensible on the second day of the course that we were asked to spend the majority of the day negotiating who were to be our partners in tutorials for the two-year programme. I thought it a foolish notion. In reality, it proved to be a huge piece of learning in terms of the understanding of relationships and group dynamics. Just as Relate had fostered the growth of group dynamics by their logistical arrangements on residential courses, so the course staff carefully fostered the growth of group dynamics from the very beginning.

This in turn provided the environment in which informal learning could take place, in the shape of personal growth and development of reflective self-awareness.

The fourth and final part of the day was taken up with participation in self-development groups. Again, this proved to be a fertile ground for learning, this time about myself. Of particular note, was my response to the authority figure of the group facilitator, which helped me to identify my ambivalence towards authority figures. Using the group as an adjunct to my personal therapy facilitated other learning. However, the greatest impact for me came during a career crisis, when the unqualified support of the group facilitator and of some of its members proved an invaluable resource. It provided me with a sense of containment and acceptance that can only come from receiving unconditional positive regard, mixed with what I call 'challenging offered with love'.

Learning from the formal learning environment

A third critical incident, which led to quite revolutionary change, was made up of three components, the first of which acted as a catalyst for the other two. I submitted a case study as my first piece of written work. I handed it to my tutor, confident that it was a truly creative piece of work, both in its manner of presentation and as a reflection of the work I had done with the client. My tutor's comments served to provide the catalyst for change. While recognizing its strengths, she intimated that I had no grasp of the difference between eclecticism and integration; that my practice was eclectic, and showed no conceptual understanding of how to develop an integrative stance.

My first piece of learning was to learn to take the criticism positively. In a style typical of my personality, I resolved to fill this gap in my knowledge, and to develop my understanding of the different metatheoretical assumptions that underlie each of the major theoretical orientations. The theory lectures provided the second and related component. Here I found myself entranced by a conceptual world, each week able more successfully to put the pieces of the jigsaw together: to marry up how theory related to practice, and indeed to show how the different theoretical orientations stood separate because of their differing underlying metatheoretical assumptions. I realized that if I was to achieve an integrative stance at a theoretical level that it would involve marrying up these different assumptions by recourse to a higher level of abstraction. I had learned what is meant by the term: dialectical thinking. Now I needed to employ it. Dialectical thinking is a philosophical system of working towards the resolution of differences that exist between factors in a particular situation. Norcross and Grencavage (1989) describe integration as 'more than the sum of its parts'. The only way forward, therefore, if I was to become integrative, was to try to resolve the seemingly opposing methodologies, rationales and visions of reality contained within each of the theoretical orientations that I employ.

This led to the third component of the critical incident: I took to reading, reading, reading! Again, it was almost impossible for a while to satiate my hunger. My 'bibles' were Norcross and Goldfried (1992) and Stricker and Gold (1993). I slowly grasped the implications of the integration debate; I searched for a personal integration which would satisfy my need to find a theoretical orientation and which would fit with my personal philosophy.

This critical incident has had immense ramifications in my life as a counsellor. First and by no means least, it led me towards a sense of being a professional therapist emerging in my own right, as I sought to marry together my personal and professional selves through the development of an appropriate theoretical orientation. I firmly believe that this can only be done by the search for, and discovery of a theoretical orientation where the underlying metatheoretical assumptions match those that underlie one's own personal philosophy (Skovholt and Ronnestad, 1995). I believe that if this does not happen, then a therapist is likely to suffer burnout or dropout. I found the answer through a process of becoming able to consciously identify and articulate my own personal philosophy for life, and finding a theoretical orientation whose underlying philosophy is consonant with my own beliefs. It is then possible to become aware of any cognitive dissonance which exists, and seek to reduce that dissonance by the enlargement or revision of the paradigm already adopted.

The growth of a mentoring relationship

Discussion of the issues outlined above led to the growth of a mentoring relationship between me and a member of staff. This proved to be a fourth critical incident. Over the next two years, this person nurtured the flowering of my abilities, of my academic self and of my counsellor self. Belief in my own competence grew dramatically through a process of introjection of another's belief in me. In the second year of the masters programme, I was to learn to own that competence. This was an important factor in my decision to leave Relate and to set up in private practice, in order to enable me to work with clients in the way in which I felt most comfortable. The learning process, which I was undergoing on the course, meant that my way of engaging in therapy changed, in line with the changes in theoretical orientation.

My interest in working psychodynamically with clients had grown from my reading of the literature, and associated with this was a growth in my understanding of how the whole process of long-term therapy enables the client to grow personally, and to integrate those cut-off parts of oneself. I wanted, now, as a therapist emerging in my own right, to help clients to grow in this way. I feel that this can only generally be achieved in long-term therapy, facilitated as it is by the therapeutic alliance that develops between therapist and client. This is how I wanted to engage with clients. This is not Relate's focus, which is to work with the adult client couple in relatively short-term, remedial work. It was, sadly but correctly, time for me to leave Relate, and to move on to another phase of my emerging professional self.

This significant development could not have occurred without the growth of my sense of self, which this mentoring relationship facilitated. For this reason alone (and there are many others), I shall always be infinitely grateful and indebted to my mentor.

Another meaningful relationship

It was a requirement of the course that trainees should undertake at least 12 sessions of counselling in the role of client. I understood that the purpose of this was twofold: first, to encourage self-development; and second, to enable one the counsellor to experience the role of being a client. There is considerable debate about whether personal therapy should be a requirement on counselling courses, and Windy Dryden, for one, remains ambivalent about its efficacy (Dryden and Vasco, 1991). The British Association for Counselling now requires all counsellors applying for accreditation to have undergone at least 40 sessions of therapy.

I, in turn, reflected upon my need for personal therapy. I had some two years previously undergone six month's counselling following a loss of someone precious in my life. In my early twenties, I had received eighteen months of therapy, which I firmly believe changed the whole course of my life. But I wondered what I needed to talk about at this point. I searched for and found myself a counsellor. I contracted for 12 sessions. As it turned out, it proved so vital to my self-development and the development of my capacity of reflective awareness that I continued to see this counsellor for two years. I regard this as my fifth critical incident. It proved invaluable in helping me to work through my attachment relationship with my mother, and to recognize my habitual 'anxious ambivalent' attachment style. I found Phyllis Kristal's *Cutting the Ties that Bind* (1993) helpful and also learned to appreciate how important it was to be in therapy.

However, the greatest learning as a client came from the process of reviewing my career role within Relate. I learned experientially, rather than theoretically, about the value of true unconditional positive regard and the way it fosters personal integration. True unconditional positive regard comes when one finds oneself accepted for the 'good' and the 'bad'. To me, it does not mean that one's 'significant other', such as a counsellor, believes that one is a good person in one's entirety; it means instead an acceptance of one's 'bad' side, not a negation of it, yet shining through it all, an acceptance of one's whole self. If another human being, whom you value highly, provides this gift, then I believe it enables a healing integration of the self to take place. I learned, through my therapy, the essence of object relations theory.

Having learned this, I found myself able to engage with clients at a deeper level, and indeed to provide them with this same healing experience. I have felt for a long time that there is one particularly crucial moment in therapy: namely, when the client trusts you sufficiently to tell you their secret. This secret can be recognized for its significance by the fact that in telling it, the client is telling you about what they perceive, personally, to be their 'baddest' side. I learned, from my own experience of sharing my baddest side, that if you can share it and still feel accepted, not rejected, and then healing in the form of integration takes place.

Learning from the 'worst clients'!

As I grew in confidence as a therapist, a challenge I faced was starting to believe that I was all-knowing and omnipotent. This brought the danger of over-involvement with clients. Marmor (1953) aptly describes this pitfall for the therapist as the tendency to grandiosity.

My sixth critical incident involved learning a lesson, never to be forgotten, in terms of my own grandiosity, from two incidents that occurred concurrently. The first was my receiving a verbal threat to my life from a client, the second was reading in *Counselling* (British Association for Counselling, 1996, p. 183) about a counsellor being murdered by a client. I learned painfully to regulate my over-developed sense of responsibility towards clients; that there *are* limits to my competence; and that there *are* limits to my responsibility. I learned that I owe it to myself, to my family, and to other clients not to give too much of myself.

Paradoxically, I have learned that giving up control, for that's what it was, enables me to work more effectively, rather than less effectively, with clients. This learning was partially facilitated by help from the formal learning environment. Themes of power and control in the counselling process emerged in both of my process reports (an audiotape of excerpts from a counselling session, complete with transcript and critique) in years one and two.

A professional and personal identity

Looking back on the whole course of my counselling training, and indeed, where I find myself today, I feel it is vitally important to achieve some sense of perspective. In order to do this, I have found it useful to employ the developmental models of both Friedman and Kaslow (1986) and Skovholt and Ronnestad (1992). The first of these focuses upon the changing relationship between counsellor and supervisor, and I have found it particularly illuminating for some years now. When I was selected by Relate to train as a counsellor, I remember only too well the early stage of excitement and anticipatory anxiety (stage one), as I became acquainted with the agency in the capacity of student. This stage ended with my first contact with my first client, some four months later. During the Relate training, I progressed through stages of dependency and identification with my supervisor (stage two), being more active but still dependent (stage three) towards exuberance and taking charge (stage four). I moved from complete lack of confidence, continual anxiety and desperate appeals for advice on case management to the emerging realization that perhaps the role of healer *did* include me, and a concomitant elevation in my sense of responsibility for my therapeutic actions and decisions.

By the end of training I perceived myself to be a healer, and was entering a stage of identity and independence. This fifth stage is best described as 'professional adolescence', in which I tended to question the authority of my supervisor, and is 'notable for the rejecting and/ or devaluing attitudes which the new therapist may direct towards the supervisor' (Friedman and Kaslow, 1986, p. 42).

Being a professional adolescent lasted, I believe, for several years until I decided, during my second year of the masters course, to enter private practice. I took the hitherto impossible decision to choose for myself a supervisor whose level of development fitted my developmental stage. I entered stage six of Friedman and Kaslow's model, calm and collegiality. I feel that I can now challenge my supervisor, and look upon him as a senior colleague rather than someone with whom I should, sometimes reluctantly, comply.

The process has been one of 'professional individuation', from becoming a counsellor in name only and doing it as the books prescribe, to internalizing the whole process of being a therapist until it has become an integral part of my sense of identity as an individual. This, I believe, is what Skovholt and Ronnestad describe as the stages of integration, individuation and integrity (Skovholt and Ronnestad, 1995). It involved a move from a need to please my professional gatekeepers to the recognition that the responsibility is mine. I have moved from almost constant anxiety to a relaxed working style. It has involved, not least, learning to be my authentic self in the therapy room. One therapist quoted by Skovholt and Ronnestad (1995) puts it well:

> I learned all the rules and so came to the point – after lots of effort – where I knew the rules very well. Gradually I modified the rules. Then I began to use the rules to let me go where I wanted to go. Lately I haven't been talking so much in terms of rules. (pp. 66–67)

This is not to say that I am not mindful of the ethics of our profession, nor of the way in which to build and maintain a therapeutic alliance, nor of the theoretical underpinnings of my practice. However, it does mean freedom, and I accept the responsibility that goes with freedom. For example, on leaving an agency to which I could turn for guidance and sense of identity, I had to learn to develop all these resources for myself in private practice.

I now believe that I am at the most critical stage of all. This is the stage of integrating my professional and personal selves. Skovholt and Ronnestad describe this as 'internalization' – that stage at which one moves 'towards a highly personalised way of functioning, a movement which can be described as a personal anchoring process' (Skovholt and Ronnestad, 1995, pp. 130–131). From the extensive reading, academic work and general writing which I have carried out during the past five years, I have become aware that this means finding a fit between my personal philosophy of living and my chosen theoretical orientation. This process has been going on for four years and I have not found it easy. But I have reached a stage where I have embarked upon further training in the theoretical orientation which I believe fits with my 'tragic' vision of reality (Frye, 1957; Frye, 1965).

Conclusion: drawing the themes together

In counsellor training, the informal learning environment is as important, if not more important, than the formal learning environment. My experience has been that the latter provides the essential underpinning for informal learning to take place. And I acknowledge the level of inspiration, support and help I received from others involved in my training, both my peers and my professional elders.

My learning has been a gradual process. This may seem a paradox, given the emphasis I have given to critical incidents. And there certainly were moments of insight and 'the penny dropping'. However, the learning required mulling over, alone and with colleagues. The fruits of one critical incident often led to another, and I became aware of unexpected connections, so that my learning had a synchronistic quality. This seems to happen so often in the field of counselling, for both clients and trainees. As mentioned above, I discovered that one gets the clients one needs. Frequently, the experience of synchronicity has helped to enlarge my learning from any one incident, and it has left me ready to believe that 'critical incidents are not accidents' (Lange, 1988).

References

Bowlby, J. (1979) *The Making and Breaking of Affectional Bonds*, London: Routledge.

Bowlby, J. (1988) *A Secure Base*, London: Routledge.

Casement, P (1985) *On Learning From the Patient*, London: Tavistock.

Casement, P. (1988) *Further Learning From the Patient*, London: Tavistock.

Cashden, S. (1988) *Object Relations Therapy*, London: Norton.

Corey, G. (1991) *Theory and Practice of Counseling and Psychotherapy*, 4th edn, Pacific Grove, CA: Brooks/Cole.

British Association for Counselling, *Counselling*, volume 7 (August, 1996) No. 3, Rugby: BAC.

Dickson, A. (1982) *A Woman in Your Own Right*, London: Quartet Books.

Dryden, W. and Vasco, A. (1991) *Dryden on Counselling*, London: Whurr.

Friedman, D. and Kaslow, N. J. (1986) 'The development of professional identity in psychotherapists: Six stages in the supervision process', in F. W. Kaslow (ed.), *Supervision and Training: Models, Dilemmas, and Challenges*, New York: Haworth.

Frye, N. (1957) *Anatomy of Criticism*, Princeton NJ: Princeton University Press.

Frye, N. (1965) *A Natural Perspective: the Development of Shakespearean Comedy and Romance*, New York: Columbia University Press.

Holmes, J. (1993) *John Bowlby and Attachment Theory*, London: Routledge.

Jacobs, M. (1986) *The Presenting Past*, Buckingham: Open University Press.

Kristal, P. (1993) *Cutting the Ties that Bind*, York Beach, ME: Weiser.

Lange, S. (1988) 'Critical incidents aren't accidents', in T. M. Skovholt and P. M. McCarthy, 'Critical incidents: catalysts for counselor development', *Journal of Counseling and Development*, 67.

Malan, D. H. (1979) *Individual Psychotherapy and the Science of Psychodynamics*, Oxford: Butterworth-Heinemann.

Marmor, J. (1953) 'The feeling of superiority: an occupational hazard in the practice of psychotherapy', *American Journal of Psychiatry*, 110: 370–376.

McLeod, J. (1993a) *Putting it Together: Personal Learning on Counsellor Training Courses*, unpublished manuscript.

McLeod, J. (1993b) *Introduction to Counselling*, Buckingham: Open University Press.

Norcross J. C. and Goldfried, M. R. (eds) (1992) *Handbook of Psychotherapy Integration*, New York: Basic Books.

Norcross, J. C. and Grencavage, L. M. (1989) 'Eclecticism and integration in counselling and psychotherapy: major themes and obstacles', *British Journal of Guidance and Counselling*, **17**(3): 227–247.

Ogden, T. H. (1992) *Projective Identification and Psychotherapeutic Technique*, London: Karnac.

Proctor, B. (1988) 'Supervision: a co-operative exercise in accountability', in M. Marten and M. Payne (eds) *Enabling and Training*, Leicester: National Youth Bureau.

Skovholt, T. M. and McCarthy, P.M. '(1988) 'Critical incidents: catalysts for counselor development', *Journal of Counseling and Development*, 67: pp. 69–110.

Skovholt, T. M. and Ronnestad, M. H. (1995) *The Evolving Professional Self: Stages and Themes in Therapist and Counselor Development*, Chichester: Wiley, p. 16.

Stoltenberg, C. D and Delworth, U. (1987) *Supervising Counselors and Therapists: A Developmental Approach*, San Francisco: Jossey-Bass.

Stricker, G. and Gold, J. R. (eds) (1993) *Comprehensive Handbook of Psychotherapy Integration*, New York: Plenum.

11

A Leap into the Known

Geof Alred

It is not every day that a university teacher with eighteen years of teacher-training experience behind him takes the step, or rather the 'leap', of starting all over again as a student. This is precisely what Geof Alred did in taking a sideways career move from being a teacher of teachers to becoming – eventually – a trainer of counsellors. In a very personal, almost intimate, way he allows the reader to see inside him, to witness the apprehension, the confusion, the vulnerability and the excitement as his familiar, academic learning was turned on its head and he became open to new ways of learning and being. Significant turning points in the process of his personal and professional transformation are highlighted and provide the basis for maxims which sum up his learning as a trainee as a conclusion to the chapter.

It is one year since I completed counsellor training. I followed a part time advanced diploma course, one day a week over two years. My training was part of a sideways career move from teacher education into counselling and counsellor training. I have worked in the same large, ever-changing university education department for eighteen years.

There are many ways to talk about the training experience and what I have taken from it. As I have gathered my thoughts in preparing this chapter, I have shifted around various themes – theory, practice, supervision, the personal, being professional, relationships on the course, relationships outside the course – and have been acutely aware that the effects of training continue to unfold. I am also aware of what from my past I brought and did not bring to training. The challenge now is to express the learning within the flow of a life and as continuing while portraying the specialness of the training experience. What follows is an attempt to do justice to all aspects of the course, to my own particular experience and to the professional and personal upshot.

I shall begin by saying that the central outcome of counsellor training was that at the end of the course I could counsel, and I regarded myself as having joined a profession, albeit a young, sometimes uncertain, one. This may sound obvious but previous training had been in counselling skills and was minimal, and I had not worked before in a formal counselling context. I had come to an interest in and commitment to counselling through working over many years with students training to be teachers, and through my own experience of life and my own personal struggles. I knew I could help, through listening, accepting, helping students gain understanding, helping them touch base, whatever base for them was. When I declared a serious interest in redeployment into the area of counselling, and sought my department's support for retraining, several colleagues affirmed my decision and I felt my capacity to help others was recognized. However, I was also full of trepidation. While there were many aspects of being a counsellor of which I can now see I was blind, I was very aware that I lacked an appreciation of the professional context of counselling, it seemed like a foreign land I was eyeing from afar. I also felt cut adrift from the core values of person-centred counselling I now espouse and associate with the 'living reality' (Connor, 1995, p. 19) of being a counsellor. Training was not a 'next step' along a clear career path but a 'leap' away from weariness and frustration with what I had been doing for a long time towards something I believed would be more fulfilling and worthwhile. I have seldom made a more right decision.

Beginning

Counsellor training coincided with other significant life changes. I was moving on from a difficult period during which my marriage ended and my family became fractured. I had not long moved house. The decision to take my interest in matters psychotherapeutic seriously had been preceded by dissatisfaction at work and with myself at work. Counsellor training requires serious attention to self and, in retrospect, I realize that I was ready for that. In parallel with external changes, I felt I was changing in myself, achieving some personal resolution and solidity. From the beginning the personal and professional perspectives have been closely intertwined. Each Friday of the course began with an early start and a train journey of about an hour. There was a 12/15-minute walk at each end. The journey, the distance and the time that separated home ground from the training environment, the train itself (usually the Transpennine Express), the stations, the streets I walked through – all of these tangible, mundane aspects of the training day became increasingly significant as the course progressed. They became symbolic of a personal journey and transition, most of all the to-ing and fro-ing between the familiar and the new. The experience of 'being between' was strong and energizing. Over the two years, an unexpected inversion took place, the familiar became distant and the new came to feel like home. Geography was stood on its head; my map for being and knowing was redrawn.

As I walked from the station to the college on the first day, I had little inkling of what was in store. It turned out to be an exciting and exhausting day of newness, arrangements, strangers, anticipation, apprehension, and fascination. I expect we were told essential information but I have no recollection of that; I took away only feelings and impressions, some enduring memories of things said, some scrappy notes I wrote and some handouts. I remember with gratitude a sign in the coffee bar – 'a Big Yorkshire Welcome'.

One trainee had yet to arrive – he eventually came in the third week. As various groups were formed – for skills training, supervision, experiential sessions – he acquired, in his absence, a fascination. What was he like, would he fit in, how would the groups work? I wonder now if in those early weeks he was the first object of projection for the group, as each of us, in our own way, arrived, introduced ourselves, began to meet others, became settled and unsettled, felt both comfortable and vulnerable, felt glad and apprehensive, began to sense the possibility of connection one with another, began to live out the commitment to training each of us had made. Were our light-hearted speculations about him the first innocent expressions of emerging commitments to one another?

Over the summer break before the course started, I read *Psycho-therapy: A Personal Approach* by David Smail (1978). Not a lot of thought had gone into choosing this for holiday reading, but it proved excellent preparation, although it was not until much later that I fully appreciated its aptness. Smail rails against aspects of academic psychology from the perspective of an experienced clinical psychologist. His incisive and elegant prose, his morality and rootedness in certain philosophical traditions added up, for me, to a powerful statement about the shortcomings of academic psychology as it relates to helping and a compelling argument for looking elsewhere for understanding and insight. Reading his book became an addiction, I did not want it to finish, it allowed me to let go, to jettison, much of my own academic baggage. It cleared the decks, created space for something new. Smail also identified what I might get hold of – notions of human agency, autonomy, responsibility, meaning, good faith, self in relationship – get hold of wholeheartedly, with feeling as well as thought. The full significance of these lessons was only glimpsed at the time, only partly known, it took two full years before they were truly learned, or rather were begun to be truly learned.

I knew intuitively it was the right book to read, far better than some 'first steps in counselling'. I needed to clear a space. As a consequence, I didn't get far with the official reading list. I tried Egan (1994), whose model of the skilled helper dominated the first year, and could not see anything other than references to social learning theory and such like, old hat stuff from my undergraduate days. I was not ready to read Egan.

Smail's book had been on my shelf for years, given no more than a passing browse. It was as if it had waited patiently and now revealed its truths and possibilities. Much of it was read on a Cretan beach, and somehow the heat, the sea air, the disconnectedness of a package holiday, amplified its significance for me. I remember vividly the incongruity of reading the final chapter on a boat and bus trip after walking the Samaria Gorge and wanting intensely to share with somebody just how helpful it was.

This kind of experience was to recur throughout the two years. Something known became known anew. The familiar became unfamiliar before becoming familiar again. At the outset, as a psychology graduate and education tutor for many years, I was familiar with theory and literature germane to counselling. Smail's book helped me gladly and properly forget most of it. My existing knowledge was partial, not holistic, and starting from it would have made learning as a trainee extremely difficult, perhaps impossible. I had to forget in order to remember. I cashed in my investment in academic psychology and opened a new account.

And more often than not new learning, new deposits in the account, came bursting into awareness through reflection of something on the outside — a book, a quote, an event, something seen or heard, a client's story, a physical place, a chance remark, a pattern, a pebble, on one occasion an overgrown lawn. Much of my experience had a synchronistic feel to it; I was constantly tripping over coincidences and felt surrounded by evidence of my own learning. Connections with and on the outside enacted connections inside, as if . . .

As we inhabit this world of ours, we amble about in a field of pregnant objects that can contribute to the dense psychic textures that constitute self-experience. (Bollas, 1992, p. 3).

I became intensely interested in the concrete, the particular, the specific, and turned my back on the general and the theoretical. By the end of two years I was beginning to understand in a totally new way the place of artistic and poetic and musical expression in human affairs, and the mythical and the metaphorical, and to believe that I too could use those forms of expression in my own communications, with self and with others. The following quote from William Blake in Robert Hobson's *Forms of Feeling* (1985, p. 161) which I came across half way through doing a small research project on metaphors in counselling during the second year, struck me with some force — it reflected my learning at that moment:

He who would do good to another must do it in Minute Particulars: General Good is the plea of the scoundrel, hypocrite and flatterer. For Art and Science cannot exist but in minutely organised particulars.

Confusion

Another feature of beginning became apparent as the first term progressed. For a while, it was confusing. We were required to keep a learning journal but I didn't write anything for the first few weeks, beyond brief notes as things occurred to me. I was also slow in arranging counselling practice. Why was this when I was enjoying the course so much? I realized later that this was actually why. I had enough to be getting on with, there was as much as I could respond to as I became accustomed to the ways of a counselling course and juggled course requirements and work commitments.

But there was another deeper reason. I think I was demonstrating to myself I could set aside the intellectual and the narrowly academic. I was suspending, more or less consciously, some parts of myself to allow space for others. My emotional self and a determination to be congruent took time to gather momentum. For a while it appeared as if nothing was happening, like an oil tanker changing direction. There was a hiatus. Talking about it with a tutor, as best I could at the time, was helpful, but I suspect the confusion was unavoidable and indeed necessary. Sometime later I came across the Gestalt phrase, from my supervisor – the 'value of confusion'. Its force now seems so obvious, an example of the observation by one of the tutors that a good supervisor tells you the obvious. But then it was quite different, it was a revelation – if you change direction, there will be turbulence. Having convinced myself and others that I had something to offer counselling, having presented myself on paper and at interview to prospective tutors, it was strange as well as exciting to live out what Smail's book was telling me – to put certain things aside, at least for the time being. I was on the threshold, not so much of something completely new, but of a re-discovery and recovery of neglected parts of myself. Embarking on counsellor training was a bewildering, exhilarating and timely leap into the known.

Learning from others – tutors

Space is a much used, mundane even, metaphor for what people often find helpful when facing new learning. However, it is an excellent description of what was offered by tutors. They created a spaciousness, a quality of space and safety that allowed for trying out, showing vulnerability, gaining direction, clarifying understanding, setting new goals. This was particularly evident in the sessions where theory was presented, where opportunities were provided for getting hold of powerful ideas, through experiential learning and discussion. One example is the simple exercise of telling another trainee how she reminded me of someone, and vice versa, to introduce and explore the idea of transference. How to develop it theoretically, and the conceptual ins and outs of transference, seemed secondary to grasping the strength of the idea of the 'presenting past', the reality and pervasiveness of that aspect of how we relate one to another and seek sense in our transactions one with another. Much of the learning, guided and gently shaped by the teaching, was like this. I came to describe it as associative – bringing together ideas and concepts and insights so that each learner linked them in their own way, hooked them into personal experience and existing understanding. Seldom did jargon, or academic overload, get in the way. This provided a solid basis for further reading and study, when I wanted to become more focused and analytical, academically and/or professionally. For years, I have envied colleagues who taught in this way, most often colleagues with a background in literature. Now it seemed I was working towards that myself, through being on the receiving end, gaining the confidence to be that sort of student, knowing in my bones that, in due course, it would be transformed into being that sort of teacher.

Two tutors ran the first day of the course. As part of their introduction each expressed a fundamental view about learning as a trainee counsellor. One quoted Carl Rogers' notion of teacher as facilitator of 'significant' learning. The other pointed to a parallel between learning on a counsellor training course and a client learning in counselling. The second of these became especially helpful in the second year, as I describe below. The first felt true throughout the two years. It is something that is easy to say and might have easily been little more than rhetoric. But it was not, a facilitating environment was created, a major element of which was encouraging each member of the group to see the group as the site of learning. This indeed happened and looking back, my memory is that in an important sense the tutors were part of the background. What was and was not on offer from them was made clear at the outset and remained so in practice. They did not intrude as teachers but were very present as people with a clear role. I was enabled to learn in, from and with the group. As a teacher myself, I have learned a lot from this, especially when tutors demonstrated counselling. Their readiness to practice what they preached, to walk the talk, chimed with my intention on the course to be as congruent as I knew how.

Learning with others – fellow trainees

The deep pleasure and challenge of training was felt most fully in working, learning and sharing with others. We were a mixed group. There were some people I took a long time to get to know, and there was no one from whom I didn't learn. Many of our discussions helped fill the space left by heeding the message of Smail's book. I don't find it easy to express how I learned as a group member, but certainly process was important, and often was very visible, such as when we scribed for each other when thinking aloud about assignments, and in group supervision. With regard to content, I was struck over and over again (and often kept quiet so that I could concentrate on listening) by what people who had considerable experience of counselling had taken from different theoretical perspectives, hearing it talked about starting from practice, people talking directly out of their situation and experience. One way to express this is to say I became more aware of the power of using ideas to shape conduct, to know what to do, rather than treating ideas as ends in themselves to be elaborately woven and admired. This is a construction I am placing on memories after more than a year, I didn't think about it in this way at the time. One thing I did say, in a personal development statement at the end of the first year, was that my fellow trainees had unwittingly re-taught me everything I know about teaching.

In my own practice and beliefs, I moved towards being a person-centred counsellor, and my impression is that the group itself became more person-centred. By chance, one Friday near the beginning of the second year, we had a day more or less without a tutor because of unforeseen circumstances. This proved fortuitous, as we slowly shifted from expecting something to be tutor-led, through disappointment towards taking control of the day and having a long serious discussion about Rogerian core conditions as a bedrock of practice that we wanted to explore further. Egan had dominated the first year and what seemed to happen on this day was a natural assertion of something important but so far unsaid by many members of the group. By coincidence (or maybe not), a new tutor who joined in the second year described himself as person-centred.

At roughly the same time, we were invited to plan the second of two residential weekends. The theme of creative techniques soon emerged and over a number of weeks a programme combining a 'return to Rogers' and various creative activities was devised. Our fun and games with paint, music, sculpting and dance took place in primary classrooms – very fitting for free children!

In all of this group experience, there seemed to be a lot of coming together and true sharing, and genuine liking among us. The new tutor commented on how supportive of each other we were and hinted at the value of being more challenging. He may well have been right, it was for the most part a friendly group, and opportunities for challenge were lost.

Here I would like to describe a part of the weekend that offered a powerful insight about counselling. The programme included a dance and mime session. After some solo mime we formed pairs, then fours, then eights and then the whole group became an untidy snake of a dance. What was special was how the pairs came together. With the person closest to me, we made contact by touching the back of each other's hand, while continuing to slowly dance. We were a couple dancing and to stay in touch required complete attention to the other and to self. The form of contact, unlike a conventional grip, was delicate, completely mutual, and of the moment – it only continued from second to second because of commitment, attention and skill by both parties. It was an extraordinary experience – a bodily demonstration that to truly listen to/know/meet another requires truly listening to/knowing/meeting self. It was magic, it was ordinary and it was utterly human. Looking back, I think the timing played a part. The exercise could have been no more than fun and interesting, but at that stage of the training, I found a secure reference point for deepening my understanding of psychological contact (Rogers, 1951), of genuine meeting within a therapeutic encounter, 'when we dare to dance with the unfamiliar other' (Anderson, 1997). A more general lesson, and one that cropped up elsewhere in the weekend, was using the body as a way into understanding, following the Gestalt insight that often the body speaks first/honestly/helpfully when exploring difficult and/or neglected psychological terrain. It was age-old wisdom smelling fresh as a daisy.

Alongside a focus on person-centredness in the second year, I felt relationships within the group become more complex. I became aware of some people working hard on personal issues (and I am sure I also remained unaware of many). Following the residential weekend just mentioned and throughout the penultimate term, there seemed to be 'psychodynamic' currents washing around. I was in the throes of my own counselling which had taken unexpected turns and I began to feel at times emotional and mildly anxious during Fridays. Sometimes when doing a round, if I was near the end the anxiety would rise to an uncomfortable level. Such experiences were interspersed in days of feeling congruent, composed, in true connection with people and fully alive. It was a strange mixture.

In this interpersonal flux and complexity, another valuable lesson was learned from observing a fellow trainee who seemed to be living out something that could easily have been my experience five, ten, twenty years ago. He seemed to swing from a basically pragmatic cognitive approach of a good problem solver to being more psychodynamic. There was a phase when everything seemed to have psychodynamic significance for him. This brought into focus an old concern – how do you know when to interpret to find meaning? Psychodynamic interpretation can come too readily, it can become a parlour game, it can be defensive, and it can be aggressive. What is the test? From a strengthening person-centred position, I concluded that there is no test, at least not one that resides solely and simply within a theoretical domain. But there is commitment to personal integrity, and there is the serious intention not to bullshit. I found these largely private reflections very instructive, it felt like real growth. I later linked it to fundamental questions about how we can be sure of anything, how to do counselling research, how we can trust what we think we know, when I came across the following helpful quote:

> The truth of statements is ultimately bound up with the intention to live the true life. (Habermas, 1970, quoted in McLeod, 1994, p. 176)

This aspect of training – relating to others in the group – is the most difficult to condense into a section of a chapter. In writing it I have been conscious of wanting to respect my fellow trainees and their experience.

Doing, being

The core theoretical model of the course was Egan's skilled helper. A large amount of time in the first year was devoted to studying and practising this model. Skills work and, as the summer term approached, the video presentation loomed large. Working with three others every week for a year to master a highly developed problem management model of counselling meant that by the end I and others had made steady progress and had clear views about the Egan model. It was not/is not how I typically counsel but as a central component of training it was highly effective. It provided a core around which to develop practice and facilitated the task of integrating other approaches.

Early skills work was very much about 'doing', of trying to be faithful to the model, and trying to help each other through the self-consciousness of using video. There was much fumbling and stumbling, and lots of laughter. I coined the phrase 'pliant client' to refer to our keenness to help the hapless trainee lost in the byways of the model. Slowly Egan was tamed and we began to feel in command. Growing competence was a curious process. It felt like the 'doing' was soaking into the skin, going inside and meeting up with personal values and a sense of self that was becoming more secure and known. Textbook interventions, however self-conscious and inept, if made in an atmosphere of trust, could be very powerful. Reflecting on my progress in the 'doing' part of training over the first year, I remembered hearing the actor Anthony Hopkins talk about preparing for a part in a stage play, that of the editor of the Russian newspaper, Pravda. He dressed as this man, took the same hairstyle and adopted his mannerisms, observed 'him' in a mirror, and slowly began to feel like him, or what Hopkins imagined he felt like, and so was able to be him on stage. I have often thought about this parallel in relation to skills training, of Egan as a bridge into enacting, hopefully authentically, a certain way of being. It was much more than that I had become able to use the 'skilled helper' model. This construction on my experience was reinforced when I read an experienced counsellor reflecting on becoming interested in psychosynthesis. She writes:

... psychosynthesis has taught me new ways of being and new ways of working – and Egan is still important to me. In fact, I have brought Egan to psychosynthesis. (Inskipp, 1993, p. 94)

The idea of taking Egan on my own journey felt right.

A leap into the unknown

If the start of the course was full of unfamiliarity, the first residential weekend, three weeks into the course, was truly the unknown. Looking back it is remarkable to have felt so ignorant and innocent. The weekend took place in pleasant surroundings, with a degree of comfort, and included a 'hidden curriculum' of laughter, games and late night singing, the genesis of a golden vein of humour that ran through the two years. What I remember most may seem like a paradox. From the start, an atmosphere of safety was created – the trust building exercises really worked. I also felt anxious. The first morning I wanted out, I felt uneasy, edgy. I felt, at that point, that I had leapt into the unknown and I wanted out. A tutor gave helpful reassurance. Writing about it later in my learning journal, the image of the big Indian in the film *One Flew Over the Cuckoo's Nest* leaping through a window to escape seemed to fit. Now, three years on, it seems an extraordinary association, and never subsequently was I reminded of the film. So often, to capture experience, I would reach for words, or an image, that out of context, and soon after, would seem too extreme, or wide of the mark. But at the time that's how it was, and the expression was the best I could do. I have often reflected on this in relation to listening to clients, as they struggle to find some fitting expression for their experience and feelings, reaching for the 'still unspeakable' (Leijssen, 1990, p. 234) as they self explore, as they take the risk to share with another. In the flow and flux of a client's experience and the counselling process, I am learning that the art of listening lies in knowing what to let pass and what to return to, what to nurture or amplify, what is truly of the moment and what will resonate and reveal if given the space. Learning to listen came out of all corners of the course, all points of the compass, but especially it came from the experiential group that gave the chance to truly listen to myself as I listened to others. By the end of the first year of the course, I was beginning to appreciate what Susie Orbach (1994) means when she talks about listening for the 'emotional veracity' of what people say.

Language

Hearing and speaking words became a major preoccupation. An early, and simple, example was the word 'however'. We were required to peer assess each other's essays. Feedback on my first essay contained some positive and neutral comments, and then a 'however ...', followed by a negative comment – it felt undermining, it cancelled out the positives. There were other examples, my favourite being 'but'. I could only hear this seemingly innocent and common little word as occlusive, denying, negating, and adversarial. There suddenly seemed to be a world of difference between, for example, 'I love you darling, but ...' and 'I love you darling and ...'. I became sensitive to 'but', disavowed it, stopped using it, was teased about this self imposed ordinance, laughed at myself about it – 'but' became public enemy number one – and all the while I knew that within this mini-obsession was some important learning. It was to do with acceptance, with acknowledging seemingly contradictory elements of others and situations, and of myself. It was part of making connections that so often seems to be what growth and insight are about. By refraining to 'but . . .' something, it can stick around and find its rightful place, creating the possibility of a sense of self that is more accepting of complexity, more known, more autonomous.

But (and I no longer discipline myself, Lent is over!) language as an important theme of training first occurred to me listening to a tutor talk about the Egan model. The two examples above may have been a defensive over-sensitivity on my part, but I don't think they were just that. The course drew attention to how we speak as counsellors. The tutor's language, for example, was clean and true, she spoke the Egan way. By this I mean that what she said was unambiguously related to what she intended to say. How do I know? My answer to this question is to refer to the model and to recall how effective 'Egan' interventions could be in taking the client forward, so that she herself begins to speak more cleanly and truly. As a trainee who weeks before could only read Egan in a narrow academic way, I found this perspective on training fascinating and helpful. I was learning a new language.

Other ways of talking elsewhere on the course were instructive too. The spaciousness when looking at theory described above was mediated through an open inviting sort of talk. In the experiential group, this was taken further. As with Egan language, I was struck by the facilitator's use of words to assist exploration and sharing, often painful difficult sharing. For months it seemed like magic. Slowly I began to notice how she spoke and in particular that she often left a sentence unfinished, offering a respectful opportunity, an open door that someone might wish to gently push. Over time, 'unfinished sentences . . .' came to epitomize facilitation that on several occasions took me, and others too, to the edge of learning and awareness, where 'it was safe enough to feel unsafe' (Walker, 1996, p. 132). I find it difficult to capture the delicacy and aptness of her words, in comparison mine here seem flat.

Given an academic interest in language, a focus on the languages used in the counselling world has been a useful way to reflect on practice. This approach would not suit everyone and I recognize language as only one of several elements that combined to make the training experience what it was. However, training has renewed an interest in words, and after many, many therapeutic conversations, I appreciate better the power of talk for:

. . . lifting experience into the somewhat higher regions of imagination and making us feel more alive (Moore, 1994, p. 199)

– and find it helpful to ponder on the following –

> Conversation performs a pleasurable and gentle alchemy on experience, sublimating it into forms that can be examined. Experience itself takes wing from conversation . . . I would reverse the notion that conversation is important because it is therapeutic, and say instead that therapy is helpful because it is conversational. To the soul the important thing is talk, not healing. (Moore, 1994, p. 199)

Becoming a client, being professional

The theme of this chapter, so far, is transition, of being 'in between' – between the old and the new, the space between a client and myself, in and among my 'company of selves' (Mair, 1977), between and among, criss-crossing busy terrain, both physical and psychological, making connections, engaging in a myriad conversations. Hence the metaphoric significance of the to-ing and fro-ing on Fridays.

However, there is perhaps another chapter to be written, overlapping with this one, about the theme and metaphor of the journey, more akin to one-way travel. Reflecting on the chronology of the two years of training, I can see how I, and others in the group, seemed to go through different phases. No doubt my/our experience followed a pattern others would recognize (Skovholt and Ronnestad, 1995). Here I shall describe one major junction on the journey. It occurred over the summer break.

In the first year, everything on the course was 'grist to the mill', the mill being a change of direction in how I choose to live my life, a change of fundamental concerns, priorities and way of being. I abandoned tired outmoded habits of thought and feeling. There was barely enough grist, the mill kept turning, night and day. However, had it continued like this, I suspect my training might have been unsuccessful professionally, or taken me away from counselling altogether. What happened, quite naturally but not without effort, some confusion and pain, was a separation of personal and professional development.

Two parallel paths opened up, one that took me to being a client, and the other to the profession of counselling. The comment by one of the tutors at the start of the course about a parallel between the counselling process and the training process became strongly felt. A potent source of learning was constant comparison, noting similarities and differences, between the two paths. At around the time of a session in preparation for doing a research project, during which the tutor had disclosed how the research project of her own training had taught her a lot about herself, I felt a shift from learning as 'un-learning' – a major theme of the first year – to a focus on the context in which I was beginning to work as a counsellor, the actual counselling service and team I joined, the professional context and the wider organizational and societal context of counselling.

At the start of the second year, I formed a new relationship with a new peer review partner, a member of the group with whom I spent 30 minutes each week discussing our respective concerns and issues to do with training. We began, predictably enough, by looking at what each of us wanted from the second year and discovered a mirror image of aspirations. She wanted to be more spontaneous, I wanted to be more focused, so jokingly but also seriously we agreed to swap goals.

The path to being a client was strewn with vivid, arresting experiences. In my learning journal, I described them as a synchronistic necklace. During the summer term of the first year, I was deeply affected by a client who presented with issues close to my own life story. He was very distressed, he raged and cried and suffered, and my eyes filled with tears. Supervision helped me become clearer about my involvement, I identified my needs and responsibilities, and clarified the challenge if I was to be helpful to him. I decided then to seek counselling for myself, but I did not decide when. The beads of the necklace were a series of events and experiences strung out over several months. They included the following: a slowly growing awareness of something bubbling up into consciousness, a newspaper article about the death in 1960 of the writer Albert Camus, tutor feedback on my learning journal about the value of personal therapy, being asked by a fellow trainee to read and discuss a book entitled *In Midlife: a Jungian Perspective* (Stein, 1994), news reports of the desecration of cemeteries in France, a particular dream, coming across again the Camus article, a meeting with someone who that day had thought of walking in a cemetery, a visit myself to a cemetery with a friend wanting to find for the first time her grandmother's grave. And then, four terms into the course, it felt the most natural thing to do, to seek counselling. Becoming a client was a highly complex, educational, challenging and helpful process – being a client was extremely helpful too.

Shadows

I hesitate to single out difficult parts of the training as a separate section. Challenge and support usually went together. However, sometimes the grist in the mill was gritty and unpalatable, and an account of the two years would not be faithful to my experience if it were relentlessly upbeat and positive. There were shadows, inevitably, there were difficulties, upsets, demands that I wasn't wholehearted in meeting. Although I probably wouldn't have said so at the time, I know that they have contributed as much as everything else to my learning.

I single out two to share here, one to do with me, the other to do with the course and me. First, I failed to appreciate the energy required to couple together a full time job and retraining. Steadily increasing tiredness became a major theme in the last third of the course. As I struggled to meet end of course requirements, other things went unattended, some important, some less so, such as my small suburban lawn. It grew and grew in the early summer warmth and soon became an unfettered meadow revealing a dozen different nodding grasses. I collected a bunch to remind me of this measure of how wrapped up I had become in doing what was required for the course. It is difficult to judge the effects of this. However, I know I felt less than present with some clients and made mistakes. Also, I found skills work hard in the second year and sometimes did not use it well. I suppressed feelings to avoid confrontation, often felt detached, could not muster energy. Tiredness that could be held at bay in other parts of the course intruded. So practice suffered. Kottler's (1993) discussion of burnout gave some reassurance.

Second, I have realized since completing the course that during those two years I did not develop a politically or sociologically critical stance towards counselling. If my training can be described as re-awakenings, opening doors and setting things in motion, one ball that did not start rolling was a rigorous and philosophical perspective on the place of counselling in contemporary lives and communities. I believe this to be essential if counselling is to be ultimately for the good, whatever direction it takes as a profession (van Deurzen-Smith, 1995). Critical, and often ill informed, newspaper articles were pinned on notice boards at college but they never impinged, they never came down onto the cushions or into the group. This may be exaggeration on my part, and I may have missed things. Certainly, the course fostered the belief that starting from ethics is a good way, perhaps the best way, to work towards good practice and to address the wider cultural and political dimensions of being a counsellor. Looking back, I realize that while Smail's book was an important stimulus in distancing myself from unhelpful aspects of academic psychology, I ignored his later work, and that of others, which challenges the efficacy and value of therapy through political and sociological analysis (Smail, 1993).

Personal development

The experiential sessions became the hub of all the connecting between parts of the course. A sense of theory, skills, relating, ethics running together was felt there, and it was the natural crossroads of all the paths to competence. Understanding congruence, for instance, or acquiring a life long commitment to learning how to listen, or coming face to face with the morality of being a professional helper, all these and many more aspects of becoming a counsellor came alive and became consolidated in the experiential group. It happened through honest sharing and a willingness to take risks. And it happened often doing quite unusual things – only once, for instance, have I ever pretended to be the water pump of a washing machine, it was truly educational, as well as hilarious.

I remember some of the comments from other trainees at our first meeting: 'I expect this to be the most important part of the course for me'; 'I'm fearful, I was in a group before when people went for the jugular, I wouldn't like that to happen again'; 'I want to find out what I'm like'. Another person cried and apologized. I don't recall what I said, but I do recall not knowing what to say, or indeed how to be. The cushions were comfy, it was the end of a long day, and I was content to look and listen. And yet after not many weeks and especially in the second year, all my learning became clear, vivid, palpable and lived in those sessions. I could see, with an inner eye, the point of it all, how the parts of counsellor training connected and fitted together, how the course structure and programme added up to a way of being, a way of living. I also experienced myself at those times as a mix of vulnerabilities and strengths, of necessities and possibilities, ever in flux. It was often hard being there, and it was hard when the experiential group came to an end.

Ending

After the rising crescendo of assessment in the summer term, the course ended abruptly, rather like Ravel's *Bolero*. It was a heady mixture of celebration and a sense of loss and grief. The weeks that followed felt full of unfinished business. It was difficult to slow down.

I shall conclude this chapter by restating that the learning continues to unfold and right now, looking back over those two years, what seems to be the most valuable learning is the following:

- The Rogerian core conditions are awesome and effective.
- I collaborate with the client in arriving at understanding. I adopt an attitude of the 'not-knowing' counsellor (Anderson and Goolishian, 1992).
- I have learned to be more imaginative and strive to help clients in 'imagining the real' (Kohut, 1997).
- Again and again I come back to the importance of listening. I am struck with the idea that a counsellor shines a 'beam of darkness' (Bion, quoted in Casement, 1985) to reveal what is normally outshone.
- Whatever else might or might not change as a result of counselling, a person makes progress if and when she/he is able to assume greater responsibility for living a life.
- Counselling is a humble activity.

These professional lessons have their counterpart in me as a person, in values, predilections and aspirations, summed up, in a rather condensed and oblique fashion, by the following:-

> ... when I became aware of myself as a welder, I became aware of myself in everything, even the way I walked. (Levi, 1988, p. 124)

References

Anderson, H. (1997) *Conversation, Language and Possibilities: A Postmodern Approach to Therapy*, New York: Basic Books.

Anderson, H. and Goolishian, H. (1992) 'The client is the expert: a not-knowing approach to therapy', in S. McNamee and K. J. Gergen (eds), *Therapy as Social Construction*, London: Sage.

Bion, W. R., *Brazilian Lectures 1*, Rio de Janiero: Imago Editora, quoted in P. Casement (1985) *Learning from the Patient*, London: Routledge.

Bollas, C. (1992) *Being a Character*, London: Routledge.

Connor, M. (1995) *Training the Counsellor*, London: Routledge, p. 19.

Egan, G. (1994) *The Skilled Helper: A Problem-management Approach to Helping*, 5th edn, Pacific Grove, CA: Brookes/Cole.

Habermas (1970), quoted in J. McLeod (1994) *Doing Counselling Research*, London: Sage.

Hobson, R. (1985) *Forms of Feeling: The Heart of Psychotherapy*, London: Routledge.

Inskipp, F. (1993) 'Beyond Egan', in W. Dryden (ed.), *Questions and Answers on Counselling in Action*, London: Sage.

Kohut, H. (1997) *The Restoration of the Self*, New York: International Universities Press.

Kottler, J. (1993) *On Being a Therapist*. San Francisco: Jossey-Bass.

Leijssen, M. (1990) 'On focusing and the necessary conditions of therapeutic personality change', in G. Lietaer, J. Rombauts and R. Van Balen (eds), *Client-Centered and Experiential Psychotherapy in the Nineties*, Leuven, Belgium: Leuven University Press.

Levi, P. (1988) *The Wrench*, London: Sphere Books.

Mair, M. (1977) 'The community of self', in D. Bannister (ed.), *New Perspectives in Personal Construct Theory*, London: Academic Press.

Moore, T. (1994) *Soul Mates: Honouring the Mysteries of Love and Relationship*, New York: HarperCollins.

Orbach, S. (1994) 'Hidden truth told by the liar'. *The Guardian* (28 May 1994).

Rogers, C. R. (1951) *Client-Centred Therapy*, Boston: Houghton Mifflin.

Skovholt, T. M. and Ronnestad, M. H. (1995) *The Evolving Professional Self: Stages and Themes in Therapist and Counselor Development*, New York: Wiley.

Smail, D. J. (1978) *Psychotherapy: A Personal Approach*, London: Dent.

Smail, D. (1993) *Origins of Unhappiness: A New Understanding of Distress*, London: HarperCollins.

Stein, M. (1994) *In Midlife: A Jungian Perspective*, Dallas, TX: Spring Publications.

van Deurzen Smith, E. (1995) *Can Counselling Help?*, School of Education, University of Durham, Occasional Paper.

Walker, M. (1996) 'Working with abuse survivors', in R. Bayne, I. Horton and J. Bimrose (eds), *New Directions in Counselling*, London: Routledge.

12

Drawing the Threads

Val Harding Davies, Kathy Hunt, Graham Davies and Geof Alred

Introduction

The chapters of this book offer a picture of the experiences of ten individuals as they reflect upon their journey through formal counsellor training. Each story is a unique account of struggles, heartaches, pleasures, excitements and personal achievements. There are also common themes. In this final chapter, we seek to provide an overview of what training can be like and what effects and outcomes it can produce. We feel it is important, however, to preface our discussion with acknowledgement of the courage and honesty with which the contributors have shared their stories. They have both modelled what is normally expected of clients and contributed to the openness and integrity that are the lifeblood of a mature, or perhaps maturing, professional community of counsellors and psychotherapists.

The courses followed by these former trainees are varied and are based upon different approaches to counselling practice. Person-centred, psychodynamic and broadly humanistic and integrative orientations are represented. In all of these, a goal of training is that trainees increase their sensitivity and understanding of themselves and others. These outcomes have, in different ways for different individuals, been achieved, and training has been a period of serious self-exploration and change. In all cases, the experiences of training and the outcomes, both professional and personal, were not fully anticipated. Training involves surprises.

This theme of unexpected experiences and outcomes runs throughout the chapters. Carol Kidd, for example, describes the course as one of the most dramatic periods of her life and suggests that training courses should carry a 'health warning'. Joan Rogers, while acknowledging the 'life-enriching' quality of training, accuses her course of having 'taken a chunk out of her life leaving her feeling older'. Hylda Taylor-Smith describes major consequences of the relentless challenges of self-analysis and self-reflection while Suzanne Keys recalls the constant pressure to continually face uncomfortable issues hitherto avoided. Van Tran acknowledges the unending challenges and also recognizes that training gave him the 'space' in which to reflect upon his personal identity. He discovered and came to terms with his 'place' among peers and clients, he found out where he belongs. Rhona Fear describes two periods of training as unique journeys each of which fostered different aspects of her professional and personal growth while at the same time bringing with them both difficulties and rewards. She describes the time between as a psychological sanctuary in which she was able to take stock, assimilate knowledge and adjust to personal changes. Nikki Kenward reflects upon how she was thrown back into earlier times in her life, revisiting the sounds and pictures from 'old tapes' that reverberated for her while on the course. She recounts the painful moments of her brief stay on her training course and describes how she used the experience to reflect on her life, regain her personal power and make the choice to leave the course. For Caroline Kitcatt, the emotional impact of training focused her attention upon her relationship with herself. She describes training as 'the best time in her life, so far'. Each trainee encountered the unexpected, in his or her own way.

There is little doubt that counselling and psychotherapy courses can have a profound effect upon the personal lives of trainees. Individual courses may differ in their theoretical, philosophical and values base but the impact of the experience of training appears to be immense, no matter what the fundamental underpinnings happen to be. 'Indifference', in our experience, has never featured in the reactions of trainees as they reflect upon their experiences of training. So what is it about the training that makes it such a unique experience? What sorts of changes does training foster? And what lessons can be learned by current, prospective and future trainees, and their trainers, from the stories of those who have taken up the challenge to train as professional therapeutic helpers?

Beginnings, motivations and individual paths

Formal training is part of a longer period of transition to becoming a therapeutic helper that may span several years. Often the motivations to enter training are unclear, are not fully known at the time, but only become clearer as the effects of training are digested and assimilated after it has finished. Varied and complex reasons, such as a desire to help others, an abiding curiosity about others and matters psychotherapeutic, or a recognition that further training will improve one's effectiveness and satisfaction in one's work, may be consciously known and articulated when applying for a course of training. However, many of the stories reveal more profound motives, arising out of movement in a person's life towards what they truly believe in and aspire to, and the desire to be more truly themselves. Charting the progress of the 'evolving professional self' of counsellors, Skovholt and Ronnestad (1995) have observed that at the transition into training, counsellors 'may know the issues in an amorphous sense, but later be surprised by the depth and specificity of the elements' (p. 22). The surprises of training come not only from what the course offers and requires but also from what trainees find out about themselves. On reflection, training turns out to be a way of bringing to life something that was always there, something dormant or undeveloped. For example, Nikki Kenward talks of being a dramatist, Suzanne Keys of finding a voice, Van Tran of picking up the gauntlet, and Geof Alred of a 'leap into the known'. For Joan Rogers and Carol Kidd, being a client themselves was a catalytic event leading to more authentic expression of self, propelling them to become counsellors themselves. There is variety in paths leading to training, but a common thread is a surfacing of needs and aspirations, some of which are known in advance and some of which only become more fully known as the training unfolds. The discovery that the profession of counselling provides, as Hylda Taylor Smith discovered with some anguish and consternation, or does not provide, as Pat Garrigan discovered, a fit between occupation and self-concept (Super, 1953; Holland, 1973), between personal and professional aspirations, becomes an important part of learning as a trainee.

This mixture of knowing and not knowing is a common feature throughout training. At the outset, it is one reason why there can be confusion and apprehension, as well as excitement, as the training gets underway. Enthusiasm and insecurity are common emotions in the early stages (Skovholt and Ronnestad, 1995). Trainees entrust themselves to the good intentions of training institutions and the structures and philosophy of the course. They can expect, quite reasonably, to work hard, and to be challenged. However, they do not know how emotionally vulnerable they might become, and, what is more, they do not know they do not know how vulnerable they might become. Seemingly innocuous beginning activities, so common to counselling courses and perhaps regarded as fairly low-key by seasoned trainers, can have a profound influence on how an individual perceives the journey ahead and prepares for it. Sitting in a circle, sharing names, or simply saying something about reasons for joining the course, can have a major impact, and set the scene for what is to come.

Learning as a trainee

The lasting impact of counsellor training lies not in the separate elements that make up the course, or even in the theoretical orientation on which it is based, but in the totality of the training experience. Several contributors comment on how they learned as trainees, indicating that one outcome is greater understanding of themselves as learners. Contrasts are made with how they had approached learning earlier in their lives, being reminded of school and college days, and how that learning now seems partial and incomplete compared with the solid achievements of counsellor training. They also comment on some of the unusual ingredients of training, as they are presented with opportunities to learn from a diverse range of activities and experiences. Some activities deliberately encourage a playful attitude, as a condition of serious learning. Joan Rogers, for example, became passionately involved in making an image of the fairy tale Snow Queen, as she explored her understanding of beauty and badness. And through happily pretending to be part of a washing machine, Geof Alred demonstrated to himself and others his own spontaneity and ability to let go of an inhibition against looking silly.

Such activities, while only a part of what fills the trainee's day, emphasize the aim of training to produce holistic learning, so that trainees work towards the integration of learning in the three main areas of skills, theory and personal development, and begin to live out their own learning as a personal counselling approach. Ostensibly, skills demonstrate competent counselling, theory is the basis of reflective practice, and personal development is the journey of increasing self-awareness and self-knowledge. However, this is too simple a division, and trainees certainly do not learn in discrete compartments. They may try to do so initially, following outmoded habits acquired in school or elsewhere, but eventually, if the training is working, there is a shift not only in what is learned but how it is learned. Geof Alred has described elsewhere the impact of a session in a personal development group on himself as a learner:

> Up until that point, course components had been experienced as relatively separate ... Gradually connections between these areas became apparent until the personal development group experience dissolved artificial barriers between them and initiated more fluid learning. Once begun, this form of learning was unstoppable; the barriers were gone forever'. (Alred, 1999, p. 258)

Embarking upon counselling training is rather like being presented with a road map, the parameters of which are defined by the theoretical orientation and specifics of the course. The terrain through which people may travel in order to reach their destination is only partially defined by the reality of the course. Although there are signposts along the way in terms of course components and requirements, the actual journey can only come alive as each individual finds their own route, and works towards being the counsellor they are becoming. As training proceeds, a demanding and engrossing individual process gathers momentum. Caroline Kitcatt describes this process by saying that 'I felt very much in touch with everything that was going on for me, in fact it became quite deafening at times'. And for Hylda Taylor-Smith, 'Attending the course each week opened up a space for self-analysis, reflection and challenge that I found at times relentless'.

A theme in the chapters that is central to learning as a trainee is the importance attached to working in groups. On some courses, time is set aside for what is called 'community group', when all trainees come together with an open agenda for shared experience. The complex layers of relationships, perceptions and communications, and miscommunications, in a large group make it a demanding, and sometimes uncomfortable, place for individuals to focus on how they perceive and relate with others. Contributors here point out how unchallenged and manipulative behaviour in the community group created feelings of unease, insecurity and 'stuckness' and that it was during this part of the course that being 'out of kilter' with others was particularly obvious and painful. Yet, they acknowledge that it was exactly this build-up of feelings that drew attention to old, defensive patterns of behaviour and instigated a determination to shift to a different way of being, towards openness and honesty. The whole group experience is also described as a time of discord, confusion and struggle and at the same time acknowledged as the time when the greatest learning about oneself in relation to others took place. The whole group constitutes the learning community of the course. It is unique. It is the place where the parameters of the learning environment lie and it is here where the personal, social, creative and transpersonal energies of all participants converge and transmute into collective and individual power and confidence.

There needs to be total commitment from all, staff and students, that difficult issues will be explored and worked through rather than buried (Mearns, 1997). Given these conditions, it is possible for this arena to offer participants moments of deep learning. In her chapter, Carol Kidd describes the experience of the large group as top of the list so far as risk, challenge and scariness are concerned. Caroline Kitcatt acknowledges the scariness and also sees it as the arena in which she began to differentiate between what was her agenda and what belonged to others. She also acknowledges it as excellent preparation for working with clients. Van Tran is emphatic about the importance of the community group time. He is adamant that there is no substitute for the learning, which can take place in this setting. Suzanne Keys attributes learning about realness, caring and sensitivity to experiences in the community group. She says it was in this no-hiding place that she truly came to accept individual difference.

There is no substitute for the unique dynamics of the community group. However, it is not the only place in counsellor training where significant learning can take place. Most aspects of training occur within a group setting of some sort and many of the authors here have acknowledged the powerful influence of group settings other than the large community one. Personal development groups, tutorial groups, skills practice groups, supervision groups have all been identified as places in which profound personal and professional development has taken place. As pointed out by Joan Rogers, it is the felt experience of expressing feelings and exposing vulnerabilities that is so important. Whether that happens in the community group or one of the smaller groups is really of no consequence. The important thing is that it happens and when it does it moves those involved forward, both from a personal point of view as well as from a professional perspective.

Pat Garrigan recounts the powerful learning, which happened for her within the confines of her small video group. As she and her fellow trainees 'stumbled and staggered' through their attempts to counsel one another, she experienced the healing power of the core conditions of person-centred counselling and she felt able to be truly herself. And Hylda Taylor-Smith describes a turning point during a practice training session involving herself and two others, and a video camera. It was here that she faced her struggles, voiced her frustrations and began anew the process of becoming a more authentic person.

Self-development and relationships

Learning as a trainee, in all its richness, complexity and challenge, is centrally learning about oneself. The contributors, each in their own way, and to varying degrees, have tackled the learning agenda that training courses set. Mearns (1997) has summarized this agenda as follows:

- the ability to develop personal learning goals
- a disposition to examine critically and systematically personal understanding, attitudes and skills
- a confidence to tolerate and learn from the uncertainty which may stem from having assumptions and attitudes challenged
- a disposition to openness to experience as it relates to the self, and an acceptance of responsibility for own behaviour and own learning
- the ability to use the products of consultation with others as a part of the process of self-appraisal
- the ability to appraise self openly and accurately

In broader terms, Johns (1996) has identified areas of personal development that counsellors need to work towards:

- identifying and exploring the uniqueness and patterning of our values, attitudes and constructs
- the elements in our personal family, relationship and educational history which facilitate or hinder our ability to feel, perceive, relate or protect/assert ourselves

- the balance of our personal strengths and limitations
- a sense of our emotional world, or capacity for intimacy with others and ability to stay separate and appropriately distanced from them
- a knowledge of our needs, our fears, our intolerances and perhaps most significant, our passions and powers, our tendencies, inappropriately, to invade or deprive others (p. 9).

Such self-development is, of course, not an end in itself, but the means whereby people become able to help others therapeutically. Wheeler has suggested being 'other' focused as the core of a definition of psychological therapy (1997, p. 124). The self-absorption that training requires and provokes needs to be tied to the ability to live out one's authenticity in relationship with others, most importantly with clients. This creates a tension with which trainees grapple, as Van Tran recognizes, 'There is no escape from the paradox of being 'alone' in our experience of 'being with others'.

Other indications of this tension are expressed when contributors discuss their changing attitudes to relationships in general. As a result of training there is a move away from superficial relating to more meaningful interactions with others that resonate with the trainee's relationship with herself or himself. Carol Kidd, for instance, says that she is less attracted to 'superficial chat', and prefers to talk with others 'on a relatively deep and personal level'. Friendships formed with other trainees become deep and valued; existing relationships are reassessed and sometimes ended. Being related to a trainee, through marriage, blood ties or friendship, can be an unsettling experience (Jensen, 1995). Rhona Fear found that training altered 'the nature of the relationships that I started to foster, and sadly, it also meant that some relationships floundered'. As her capacity to establish relationships of 'intense emotional intimacy' has increased, she has had difficulty with more run-of-the-mill dealings with others.

The tension between 'self' and 'other', between being separate and connected, heightened by the training experience, is also a theme of the biographies of established therapists (Dryden and Spurling, 1989). Here, a sense of isolation, recognized often as beginning in childhood, is linked with a curiosity about relationships, empathy, and a drive towards personal integration. Training can concentrate and accelerate a 'journey towards wholeness' (Spurling and Dryden,

1989). It is the process of encountering the self in so many aspects of counselling training that creates the potential for training to be a highly significant and indeed transforming episode in a person's life. The self-discovery process is relentless. Whether appraising theory, writing essays, keeping a personal journal, or engaging in the many practical aspects of the course, it makes little difference, the whole experience amounts to a continuous focus on the self, the paradoxical prerequisite for claiming the professional authority to focus on others when in distress.

Counselling

People enter training from a wide variety of backgrounds, and with varying degrees of experience of working with clients. This contributes to the richness of the interpersonal nature of training, and determines the diverse challenges and priorities that face each individual as a counsellor. Whatever each person brings, client work is new precisely because it is part of training, and it is accompanied by a heightened sense of practice as a central arena for learning on the course. There is, quite understandably, apprehension and anxiety. Being acutely aware that one is still learning, and publicly so, there are concerns about being good enough and knowing what to do. A striking feature of the chapters of this book is that the concerns individuals took into therapy sessions were closely linked to issues of personal development being addressed in all areas of their training. This is perhaps not too surprising, but it emphasizes again the importance of self-understanding and self-acceptance as prerequisites to being of benefit to clients. Contributors speak of 'being myself', 'healing involves me', and being able to 'see' clients accurately as a consequence of being able to 'see myself' accurately. The pervasive preoccupation with oneself is the heart of training; it certainly is not a side issue, nor an indulgence.

There is tension between being a learner and a counsellor, in being a beginner who is taken in good faith by the client as a competent professional. Living with this tension and reducing it produces powerful learning. The threads of training are woven into an emerging approach to practice rooted in the counsellor's deepest and strongest beliefs about himself or herself, others, relationships and what is truly of value in being a human being. Two outcomes are the conviction that counselling works and that one never stops learning about being the counsellor one is.

Conclusion

Training touches upon the whole of a trainee's life. Just as it casts trainees back into earlier times of their lives, through both reflection and regression, and provides potential to re-cast the meaning of their lives so far, so too the training is carried forward. Trainees taste, touch, feel and smell aspects of being a counsellor that will preoccupy them, in one or another, for years to come. The public, formal and structured map provided by the course is replaced by, or overlaid by, a personal, more private, map that forecasts and shapes a way ahead. Indeed, successful outcomes to training include the decision not to be a counsellor.

In this chapter, we have highlighted what we believe are defining features of the experience of counsellor training: the transition into training, the nature of learning as a trainee, and the consequences in terms of self-awareness, self-knowledge and a move towards authenticity. We have not attempted a commentary that exhausts all aspects of the contributors' stories. This might have included perceptions of technical competence; relationships with trainers; use of supervision; the sheer weight of the demands of training, both emotional and physical, within otherwise busy lives; and more detailed discussion of counselling practice and working with clients as a trainee. We have sought to provide a bridge between accounts of training by trainers that emphasize the rationale, curriculum and requirements of training (e.g. Connor, 1994; Bor and Watts, 1999; Mearns, 1997; Dryden and Thorne, 1991; Bor and Palmer, 2001) and the stories and voices of recently qualified trainees.

Completing a course of formal training is not the end of learning, nor indeed is it likely to be the end of training. Continuing professional development is an important part of being a counsellor, in order to maintain and enhance competence in a profession that can drain personal resources and resilience (Cushway, 1996). From an examination of research evidence, McLeod (1998) has summarized current views of counsellor effectiveness. He suggests a composite model consisting of six distinct areas of competence:

- Interpersonal skills
- Personal beliefs and attitudes
- Conceptual ability
- Personal 'soundness'

- Mastery of technique
- Ability to understand and work within social systems

While this list is open to discussion and further research may lead to its revision or modification, it represents a generalized picture of the competent counsellor that would be widely recognized by trainers, trainees, clients and employers of counsellors. The novice counsellor in training stands somewhere between this description-cum-vision and professional training requirements, the reality of particular courses, and the exigencies of training. It would be foolhardy to comment on the competence of the contributors they have spoken for themselves. What is clear is that in both preparing this chapter, and in the accounts of the contributors, there is a challenge to appreciate the significance of experience that is still being digested and holds the potential of further learning. We have referred above to stories of established therapists (Skovholt and Ronnestad, 1995; Dryden and Spurling, 1989) and return to this to allude to a broader and deeper context within which to assess not only the training experience but also writing about it, as the contributors have done. Skovolt and Ronnestad (1995), on the basis of interviews with 100 therapists spanning thirty years of practice, describe a stage model of the 'evolving professional self' in which a major theme is a move towards personal authenticity and integrity. The contributors to this book have taken an important step in this process. Spurling and Dryden (1989) argue that a preoccupation with self, one's inner world, self-discovery, and dealing with unresolved issues, is more than an inevitable consequence of what training offers and demands. It may also be a 'counterweight' to all the 'doing' that training involves, and an expression and recognition that in being a counsellor, what counts is just that, the 'being', 'how we are' rather than 'what we do' (Guy, 1987; Kottler, 1986).

A second major theme in the lives of established therapists is the acquisition of a personal language for expressing becoming and being a therapist, of being able to accurately and convincingly tell one's story. In undergoing formal counsellor training, and in writing about their experience, the contributors have done something similar. They have striven to express the insight that the heart of counselling is the person of the counsellor, not the techniques or interventions of any particular therapeutic approach. The accounts of their training are therefore intensely and necessarily personal, being both descriptive of and contributing to the discovery and cultivation of a professional self that can be sustained and deployed in the therapeutic process. At the close of training, these themes, evident both over the life span of therapists and the relatively short period of formal training, may be taken as confirmation that training has been worthwhile and is central to becoming a person competent to counsel.

References

Alred, G. (1999) 'A Trainee's Perspective', in R. Bor and M. Watts (eds) *The Trainee Handbook*, London: Sage.

Bor, R. and Palmer, S. (eds) (2001) *A Beginner's Guide to Training in Counselling and Psychotherapy*, London: Sage.

Bor, R. and Watts, M. (1999) *The Trainee Handbook*, London: Sage.

Connor, M. (1994) *Training the Counsellor: An Integrative Model*, London: Routledge.

Cushway, D. (1996) 'New Directions in Stress', in R. Bayne, I. Horton and J. Bimrose (eds) *New Directions in Counselling*, London: Routledge.

Dryden, W. and Thorne, B. (1991) *Training and Supervision for Counselling in Action*, London: Sage.

Dryden, W. and Spurling, L. (eds) (1989) *On becoming a psychotherapist*. London: Tavistock/Routledge.

Guy, J. D. (1987) *The Personal Life of the Psychotherapist*, New York: Wiley.

Holland, J. L. (1973) *Making a Vocational Choice: A Theory of Careers*, Englewood Cliffs, NJ: Prentice-Hall.

Jensen, K. (1995) 'The stresses of counsellors in training', in W. Dryden (ed.), *The Stresses of Counselling in Action*, London: Sage.

Johns, H. (1996) *Personal Development in Counsellor Training*, London: Cassell.

Kottler, J. A. (1986) *On Being a Therapist*, San Francisco: Jossey-Bass.

McLeod, J. (1998) *An Introduction to Counselling*, Buckingham: Open University Press.

Mearns, D. (1997) *Person-Centred Counselling Training*, London: Sage.

Skovholt, T. M. and Ronnestad, M. H. (1995) *The Evolving Professional Self: Stages and Themes in Therapist and Counsellor Development*, Chichester: Wiley.

Spurling, L. and Dryden, W. (1989) 'The self and the therapeutic domain', in W. Dryden and L. Spurling (eds), *On becoming a psychotherapist*, London: Tavistock/Routledge.

Super, D. E. (1953) 'A Theory of Vocational Development', *American Psychologist*, **8**, 185–190.

Wheeler, S. (1997) 'Achieving and Maintaining Competence', in I. Horton and V. Varma (eds) *The Needs of Counsellors and Psychotherapists*, London: Sage.

Appendix

The concluding chapter of this book summarizes the experiences of ten former trainees. The themes that emerge are the sections of the chapter, and we use them again here to offer encouragement and modest guidance to anyone contemplating or undergoing training, or reflecting upon completed training.

There are many models of counsellor training, and one thing is common to all, that while someone is involved in the process there is inevitably the parallel experience of living the rest of one's life. The significance of this obvious point is often overlooked; our everyday 'taken for granted' experiences are actually part of the richness of becoming a counsellor. We encourage you to value everything you do and everything that happens in your life while you are a trainee as opportunities to learn more about being a counsellor, and yourself as a therapeutic helper, and to notice and value the interplay between your own life and the training. The opportunities are infinite and varied. Often the learning arising from training experiences is not apparent straightaway, but comes with reflection some time later. Cultivating a reflective stance towards your experience in general will repay you handsomely. There are numerous activities that will help you do this:

- Counselling supervision
- Conversations entered into with an open heart and mind
- Creating and keeping a journal or diary
- Being imaginative: doing anything that stimulates and uses your imagination
- Reading around the counselling literature, beyond reading for specific purposes (such as writing an essay), including professional and academic journals, for up-to-date practice, theory and research
- Being balanced in your approach to combining training with the rest of your life.

Beginnings, motivations and individual paths

As you focus on the course – applying, starting, and settling into the training group – it is important to think about the resources you have that will sustain you during this important transition in your personal and professional life. You are likely to find that for the duration of the course, and possibly beyond, you will draw upon close and solid relationships, and welcome opportunities for free time when you decide just what it is you want to do, be it something stimulating and energizing, or something quiet and calming.

As training unfolds, you may well discover reasons for training other than those originally in your mind and declared in your application. You may come to appreciate that your motives are complex and multi-layered. A common theme in training is increasing clarity and understanding about why a person wants to become a counsellor. You may find that this is an important dimension of your learning throughout the duration of the course and beyond, rather than just something known and stated at the outset. Training is as likely to surprise with a deeper understanding of motives as it is to confirm (or question) original con-victions to train.

The training will present the trainee with two apparently contradictory aspects: each trainee shares the common experience of being a member of the training group, and also develops in a unique way, responding to their own needs and aspirations. So you will have the sense of being in company and separate, you will walk your own path. As you become increasingly aware of both the common ground of the training group, and your own unique path, you will appreciate that the training group is an excellent environment in which to learn about establishing and sustaining and ending the kinds of relationships that are beneficial to clients and counsellors in practice.

Learning as a trainee

Learning as a trainee often involves learning about learning itself, in that the habits and approaches acquired in the family, school, college, the workplace, or wherever, need to be questioned, added to, revised, and incorporated into a way of learning appropriate to being a counsellor. We often stick with what we know, with the familiarity of our own learning style, because we feel safe with it, and, for the trainee, it provides some stability amidst the newness of the training course. However, training involves taking risks. Before becoming competent, there will be times when you feel incompetent. This is unavoidable. What is important is how you use such experience to grow and develop. Two ingredients will help. One is feeling safe, and the other is courage. All members of the group, both trainees and trainers, can contribute to an atmosphere and working environment marked by mutual respect and support, within which trainees can take the risk of learning new things and learning in new ways.

Self-development and relationships

Counselling and counsellor training are about change. If you embark on the path to becoming a counsellor, then necessarily you will be involved in activities and experiences that are therapeutic for yourself, and you will change. Change is to be expected. Training is a place where you can really get hold of this idea, and often it is a gradual awareness that comes from the evocative and provocative experience of training. An important area of change is how you relate with others, and this sometimes involves challenge and struggle, and asking hard questions about what you want from and in relationships.

Counselling practice

Counselling practice brings together all aspects of the training, and puts them to the test. For trainees with little experience, there are naturally anxieties and apprehensions. It is important not to deny these and forfeit invaluable opportunities for learning from practice, it is important to ask for help. In any placement, the support and model provided by an experienced counsellor or counselling team will ensure that the trainee receives suitable referrals and adequate support.

Conclusion

Being a counsellor is a powerful and responsible position and also brings many rewards. There can be great satisfaction in helping another person through personal difficulties.

Being allowed into the private worlds of people in distress and confusion is a privilege. It is both respectful and wise to temper the powerfulness of offering therapeutic help with humility in the face of human suffering. Such an attitude will help the trainee to remember that learning to counsel never ends. And such learning as counsellors achieve through training can become a significant part of the stories of their lives.

Further reading

BACP, *Training in Counselling and Psychotherapy Directory 2003*, Rugby: British Association for Counselling and Psychotherapy.

Bor, R. and Palmer, S. (eds) (2001) *A Beginner's Guide to Training in Counselling and Psychotherapy*, London: Sage.

Bor, R. and Watts, M. (1999) *The Trainee Handbook*, London: Sage.

Cottrell, S. (2003) *Skills for Success: The Personal Development Skills Handbook*, London: Palgrave Macmillan.

Cross, M. and Papadopoulos, L. (2001) *Becoming a Therapist: A manual for personal and professional development*, London: Brunner-Routledge.

Dryden, W., Horton, I. and Mearns, D. (1995) *Issues in Professional Counsellor Training*, London: Cassell.

Dryden, W. and Spurling, L. (1989) *On Becoming a Psychotherapist*, London: Tavistock/Routledge.

Karter, J. (2002) *On Training to be a Therapist: The Long and Winding Road to Qualification*. Buckingham: Open University Press.

McMillan, M. and Clark, D. (1998) *Learning and Writing in Counselling*, London: Sage.

Progoff, I. (1975) *At a Journal Workshop*, New York: Dialogue House Library.

Rainer, T. (1978) *The New Diary*, New York: Penguin.

Schapira, S. K. (2000) *Choosing Counselling or Psychotherapy Training: a practical guide*, London: Routledge.

Skovholt, T. M. and Ronnestad, M. H. (1995) *The Evolving Professional Self: Stages and Themes in Therapist and Counselor Developmen*, Chichester: Wiley.

Index